OMG

a quest for God, or no god

Ruth Schleppi-Verboom
David Verboom

ISBN-10: 1977986404
ISBN-13: 978-1977986405
LCCN: 2017915784
CreateSpace Independent Publishing Platform, North Charleston, SC

ii

To the Seekers and the Finders.

The important thing is not to stop questioning.
Curiosity has its own reason for existing. One
cannot help but be in awe when he contemplates
the mysteries of eternity, of life, of the marvelous
structure of reality. It is enough if one tries merely
to comprehend a little of this mystery every day.
Never lose a holy curiosity.

—Albert Einstein

I'm pretty sure there's a lot more to life
than being really, really, ridiculously good looking.
And I plan on finding out what that is.

—Derek Zoolander in Zoolander (2001)

CONTENTS

OMG
Oh my God!

A big group of kids walks hand in hand. School's out,
and they skip and run with happy innocence. Little kids,
probably not older than kindergartners, with huge
backpacks, look at me and smile. I'm the foreigner, the
weirdo. One leaves the group, climbs on a box placed
against a wall, and opens a window. He crawls through
the window, into a house, head first, big backpack last.
Must be part of their game, I think, as I walk farther
toward my friend's house. My friend has a rooftop
terrace with a view of the city. We climb the stairs, tall
and narrow, and almost out of breath we step out in the
bright and warming sun. The view is spectacular, and for
a moment I forget my fear of heights. I see mountains,
valleys, and houses, and looking down I see a street.
Once a very busy street, my friend tells me, a main street

---

[1] Friedrich Nietzsche was a German philosopher who lived from 1844 to
1900

with traffic and shops and buses and markets. Shuhada street was the main road to the Cave of the Patriarchs, a holy place for many religions. Today there's just a handful of people strolling on the street, not much going on. Until they see us. They shout, and raise their arms. I smile and wave back. They show their fists. "Go home. We don't want you here!" I'm in Hebron, Palestine—or Hebron, Israel, depending on who you talk to. Arabs and Jews fight for the same land. After too many riots and killings on this busy street, one of the groups decided to deny access to the other group. This means that some lost their livelihoods, and others lost access to their own front door (thus the kid entering his house through a back window). For all it means restricted access to the Cave of the Patriarchs. Abraham, Sarah, Isaac, Rebecca, Jacob, and Leah are all buried here, godly men and women. I move away from the edge, out of sight. I feel dejected and hurt, and the height scares me. I want to leave. If this is God, I'm done.

A Maserati, a Ferrari, a Lamborghini, a couple of Teslas and a fourteen-dollar cupcake. We're on Rodeo Drive in Beverly Hills, California. I like to bring our visitors to Rodeo Drive, our 'pride and joy'. With anticipation we go, thinking of all things pretty and beautiful. This is the place where you will find the latest coveted shoes, watches, and necklaces in the whole wide world! The store windows are inviting (kind of), the boobs are perky (plastic surgery forever!), the pets are mini, and the cars are ridiculously expensive. We sit down with our cupcakes and watch. People watching is what we do, with the Californian sun and palm trees watching over us. As we take the last bite of our cupcakes we're fully aware of the restless rat race underneath this cover of perfection. The fear of missing out on more and better and happier and younger is tangible. Some say the god of the West is possessions and youth. I say Rodeo Drive must be his sanctuary, and if this is God, I'm exhausted.

A few years ago, Kluun, a best-selling Dutch author, wrote *God's a Fool*, a book on atheism. He explains how atheism is growing in Holland, and how the influence of the media plays a big role in this. "Fourteen percent of all Dutch claim there's absolutely no god or higher power and is atheist. It was my impression that those 14 percent were all journalists," writes Kluun in *God's a Fool*. It's true, atheism is in, and god is out. Fourteen percent might seem like a small number, but compared to the United States' 3.1 percent, it's huge. A big leap for the Dutch. You see, the Netherlands (also known as Holland, and the language is called Dutch and so are the people—how confusing is that?) once was a strict Calvinistic nation, driven by religion, dogma, and guilt. In the last few decades, most Dutch made a 180-degree turn of liberation, and Holland is now known for her liberal views. Freedom of religion is a big deal in this tiny land, and an inherited belief in God—passed on from one generation to the next—is just not cool. So, if I think there's a god, I must be in denial.

On my shoes, my pants, the streets—there's orange dust everywhere. Even the mud in the gutters is orange. Call me crazy, but I love the smell of orange dirt and love walking the streets of Nairobi. I greet the guard who stands in front of my neighbor's house, I buy a banana from the lady who sits on a paper sack, and I resist the urge to pet the puppies sold by the stoplight. It's busy, loud, and dusty on my way to the mall. One of the rare luxuries I allow myself here in Africa is a coffee at the mall each Friday. Every time I enter those sliding doors,

I walk into an oasis of peace. Air-conditioning, elevator music, no honking, and the best cappuccino you can dream of! I am happy in Africa. I love the people, the culture, and yes, the cappuccinos in the Westgate mall. Years later, back in the West, I watch the news in horror. A group of terrorists opened fire in the Westgate mall. My Westgate mall! On the tv I recognize the coffee shop, the sliding doors, the stairs. The mass shooting results in sixty-seven deaths, and more than 175 people are reportedly wounded. A religious group claims the attack as its work. If this is God, I'm sick of it.

And then there's the time I was trying to get home in Malibu, California. The street was super busy, lots of cars and paparazzi, and I wonder what the commotion is about. I live close by a Hindu temple, and it turns out Britney Spears was in *da houzz*, the Hindu house that is, for a ceremonial blessing of her sons. A big day. The Hindu priest is my neighbor, and as good neighbors often do, we talk over the fence. We talk about our goats, the weather, the cable company, and sometimes about God. One time I asked him what he thinks of God. He tells me he loves God, any god. And, he continues, while nodding his head, there are many, many gods to love. With a bright smile, he says: "If you only love one god, you can be wrong, but if you love all gods, you'll always be right!" Oh God, if there are so many of You, I'm confused.

These are a handful stories from the places I've lived. And when I say I, I mean we—David and Ruth, brother and sister. Growing up we didn't move around much but lived on the same street in Rotterdam, the Netherlands, for many years. Our mother instilled a love for traveling in us, and it has brought us all around the world. We've lived, worked, and traveled on all continents, and in at least sixty different countries. In our wanderlust, we met people from all different cultures, backgrounds, colors, and religions. It's fascinating and inspiring to see their lives and to learn from them. But many times, we found ourselves in awe, confused, upset, in denial, exhausted, or done when it came to all the religions, and we realized so did most all the other people we met. Religion and all the god-talk seems to do that to us.

So, one fine day not too long ago, David (in Jerusalem) picks up the phone and calls his favorite[2] sister Ruth (in California). David said: "Let's write a book," and Ruth said: "OK!" And so they did. What you'll find on the next pages is a combination of our stories from all over the world. And for the record, from now on we—David and/or Ruth—will be *I* or *me*. Very much like the Queen of England and the majestic plural —the royal "we,"[3] just the other way around.

---

[2] Let's keep that between you and me, the whole favorite-sister thing, and not tell the other five siblings.

[3] As Queen Victoria once so famously said: "We are not amused."

FAITH ≠ RELIGION
Give me that ol'-time religion

Silence is the language of god, all else is poor translation.
—Rumi[4]

One more thing before we get started: this book is *not* about religion. Don't give me that ol' time religion stuff. In times of iPhones, Instagram, Netflix, and Amazon, nobody's got time for that! Besides, religion has been in the spotlight way too long. All the horrible things happening in the name of God? Lost girls in Nigeria, terrorist attacks around the world, millions of refugees from Syria. Pain, horror, and terror—it seems inevitable when we turn on the news. And even worse, it's nothing new: crusades in the twelfth century, sex scandals in the church, crisis in the Gaza Strip, genocide in Bosnia, honor killings, 9/11, mass graves in Rwanda, self-righteous homophobes, suicide bombings, and the list goes on and on. It ain't pretty. Horrific deeds, justified in

---

[4] Rumi was a Persian poet, jurist, theologian, and Islamic scholar (1207–1273)

the name of a god. Any god, for there's no religion that can wash its hands in innocence. People have been killed, lives ruined, families divided, and nations torn apart.

I want to talk about God, all kinds of gods, except the god of religion. You see, religion has little to do with God—any god! Religion has become a product of a narrow mind, pride, and intolerance. Arrogance, disguised in the name of a god. Pure human fuckery, says King. And Mansionz sings: I wanna believe in religion, but nobody reminds me of God[5].

But wait a second, you might say, isn't religion based on a god? True. It once was; in its earliest and purest form, religion was based on a god, an ideal, a leader. Basically, religion is the belief or faith in a higher power. Yet the word *religion* has gotten an ugly sound to it. When I think of religion, I think of the system and how it has evolved through time and generations (and a couple of headstrong fools). I don't want anything to do with that.

When the system speaks louder than the faith—and you often see that when more regulations, traditions, and diversions emerge—it becomes an inflexible, intolerant institution. More laws, bylaws, rules, and prejudice, less god and spiritualism. Spirituality and religion were once almost synonymous, but over time, it seems that they have little to do with each other.

---

[5] *Nobody Knows* - song by Mansionz (featuring Soren Bryce)

THAT
WASN'T
ANY
ACT OF
GOD

THAT WAS AN ACT OF PURE HUMAN FUCKERY

-Stephen King, *The Stand*

Spirituality is a quest for god, for a higher power, an earnest seeking to be closer to a god or an entity. This quest results in depth, insight, mindfulness, and humbleness. This is in opposition to religion, which uses the same god or higher power to fulfill one's own agenda or goals, which unfortunately leads to a shallow, arrogant, fanatic intolerance. Duh. Watched the news lately? Depth, mindfulness, and humbleness opposed to arrogance, fanaticism, and intolerance.

Dr. Richard C. Halverson (1916–1995), chaplain to the US Senate, illustrated it so well in a speech in 1984: "Christianity started out in Palestine as a fellowship; it moved to Greece and became a philosophy; it moved to Italy and became an institution; it moved to Europe and became a culture; it came to America and became an enterprise."

You probably can tell by now I don't care for religion. Working in places such as Chechnya, Sri Lanka, the Sudan, Rwanda, the Middle East, and the Congo has only vindicated this. Each of these countries are torn apart by religion. I've seen the desolate pain, the scattered families, and the intolerance religion brought to mankind. And again, I'm not here to cast blame on one religion, for fanaticism and intolerance can be found in any religion and philosophy: fundamentalist Muslims, narrow-minded Christians, fanatic atheists, militant Jews, stubborn agnostics, and ignorant Buddhists,[6] just to name a happy few.

---

[6] These adjectives and nouns can be mixed and matched to your heart's desire.

I WOULD RATHER BAN RELIGION COMPLETELY

even though there are some wonderful things about it. I love the idea of teachings of Jesus Christ and the beautiful stories about it, which I loved in Sunday school. I collected all the little stickers and put them in my book.

The reality is that organized religion doesn't seem to work.
It turns people into hate-ful lemmings and it's not really compassionate.

— SIR ELTON JOHN

Elton John can do without religion and John Lennon sung that it isn't hard to imagine, a world without. I don't think it's that easy, because religion has been such a big part of our culture, throughout the ages. But try to imagine, for John and Yoko's sake, a world without religion[7]. Nothing to kill or die for, they say. No religion. And all its ramifications gone. From now on let's talk about spirituality, faith, and belief.

Atheists, Buddhists, Christians, Lennon, you and me—we all believe in something. There has not been a single soul I met who wasn't looking for meaning and believed in something. I guess it comes with the package—the package of being human, that from infancy on we have an innate sense that there is something more than just us. And with the sense comes the drive to discover what it might be. Whether it's a god, no god, a doctrine, a guru, or yourself, there's more.

You might be the cynic, the one to tell me you don't believe in anything. And I will be the realist to tell you that you do.

There's no proof for anyone's beliefs, *any* of our beliefs. If you want proof, better put this book down. Now. I'm not here to prove anything, but I'm stirred by the quest, the urge to explore with you, and whether this belief is in a god, the NFL, Dr. Phil, a guru, or yourself is up to you.

---

[7] *Imagine*, written by John Lennon, 1971.

like tides on
a crescent sea-beach
when the moon is
new and thin,

into our hearts
high yearnings
come welling and
surging in -

dome from
the mystic ocean
whose rim no root
has trod -

some of us call it
l o n g i n g,
and others call it
G o d

— William Herbert Carruth
American educator and poet 1859-1924

COEXIST

Dig deep

We need to respect values that allow everyone to practice his or her faith, but in the frame of our common rules of secularism.

—François Hollande[8]

The Buddha in all his wisdom said that in the search for water it's better to draw one deep well, instead of a couple of shallow ones. I'm all for the Buddha's digging deep…but only if you know where to dig. If you don't have a clue, explore. You should poke around, ask questions, and figure out which well(s) are worth digging for. It will save you from disillusionment, disappointment, and a herniated disc. Shallow one-foot wells. For now.

Or…I could tell you about my well and why it's important to me. Just take it from me, and you won't have to dig at all. Everything will be solved in one chapter, and I will hand you my ladder and happily we'll go six feet deep. Or if you don't like mine, you can take someone else's ladder; I bet you have plenty of other

---

[8] Francois Hollande was the president of France from 2012 to 2017.

people in your life with convincing ways to entice you to their truths.

Don't.

Please don't.

Don't take someone else's ladder. It has no meaning. The journey of digging and questioning can be very frustrating, but it has a purpose. Skipping this part will rob you of the depth and will leave you paddling in the shallow one-foot wells.

For many years, I knew it all. At least that's what I thought. I had found my well, plunged in, and was convinced there was only one. It worked well, although I didn't get there on my own—I was able to copy and say what others did. There was nothing forced, and it wasn't stupid because these were people I admired, and I wanted what they had. But when the going got tough, I had not questioned enough, and had not dug deep for myself. The walls of the well collapsed, and my depth had no foundation because it was pretty much based on other people's ideas. An inherited belief. So, I had to go backward and start digging those one-foot wells. I did that by asking the people I met and considering their truth with an open mind. The different cultures and traditions broadened my mind, made me milder, and somewhat wiser. I met beautiful people, each with a story to tell. Buddhists, Muslims, atheists, Jews, Christians, and so many other god-seekers and non-god-seekers, whatever —it was the stories that brought us together. We did not always agree, but we were all looking for the truth with an earnest integrity. So instead of starting with my story, I would rather take you on a journey. A journey to the different wells, and what they taught me. Then it's up to you to dig deeper. For the one who digs seeks, and the one who seeks will find.

If you want to draw water, do not dig six one-foot wells. Rather dig one six-foot well.

-The Buddha

I have also found that most people with an inherited faith, who use other people's ladders, have little tolerance toward people from other wells. Of course, I can't generalize this, but I have found that people who have a set of beliefs only based on traditions, culture, or upbringing have less tolerance and wisdom toward other believers. The other way around is true too. People who have dug and found truth for themselves are often milder and more open-minded toward others. They are secure in what they have found, and they don't need to hammer it into you to convince you, but rather have a dialogue. They coexist.

In the middle of the rocky Middle East, you find the solid kingdom of Jordan. For many years, Jordan has been a unique model of tolerance and coexistence. In 2016, they welcomed more Syrian refugees than any other country in the region and proved to be a safe haven for all religions. By law, the king of Jordan should be Muslim, and the national religion is Islam. This is very common in the region, no big deal, but unlike other countries here, Jordan is not ruled by extremists, but by a loyal and open-minded government that not only accepts but also promotes other religions. When I lived in Jordan I was stunned to see how the government supports the development of Christian schools and churches in strong Islamic areas. Not the path of least resistance if you ask me, yet it is a well-thought-out decision to bring balance to villages and communities—a great example of how "coexist" works. For this relatively small kingdom, bordered by countries of great conflict and civil wars, is an oasis of order and peace.

In Amman, the capital of Jordan, I attended a summit chaired by Prince El Hassan bin Talal, the brother of late King Hussein and uncle of King Abdullah II. Leaders and representatives of the United Nations (UN), European Union (EU), the Arab League, and the Organization of Islamic Cooperation (OIC) were all present. A room full of hotshots and me, star-struck and in awe of the combined value of culture, wisdom, and experience! On the agenda that day: 'Ethical Values and Standards in Humanitarian Aid Work, a discussion to stand together against poverty, scarcity, violence and extremism.' I wish I could tell you we solved it all that day, the world's problems and then some. We would have made a whole lot of history. We didn't—obviously—but you should have seen us! Instead of stubbornness and egos, it was all about connection, respect, kindness, and solidarity. We didn't agree on everything, and were culturally so very different, but there was a dialogue. Open and honest! Coexist.

It was the opposite of all the hurt, the hardness, and the hopeless fanaticism we see too often around us. That day, at the big long table in Amman, it was a day of hope and respect and coexist.

FUNDAMENTALISM AND SUICIDE KILLINGS ARE PART OF A **HATE** INDUSTRY. THE ONLY WAY TO END THIS IS BY **HELPING** THE PEOPLE, ESPECIALLY THE POOR.

-Prince El Hassan Bin Talal

Respect is a huge deal, we can all agree on that, but I need to add that respect is not the same as tolerance. It's so much deeper than that. There's this growing trend here in California where we show off in tolerance. We so badly want to be politically correct. That's why we're not sending Christmas cards anymore and why Starbucks red Christmas cups have caused so much controversy. Now we are wishing one another "Happy Holidays"—as if it's the next best thing. Happy Holidays! What does that even mean? Nothing really. You won't get a "HH" card from me.

A friend of mine has a friend (yes, it's one of those friend-of-a-friend stories...) who sends the friend's children Christmas presents every year. Last year the friend (of my friend) politely asked her to write *Happy Kwanzaa* on the boxes. And so she did. Lovely. Neither of them celebrate Kwanzaa, but in their zealousness to be tolerant to all, they included Kwanzaa in their repertoire. Another friend of mine celebrates Hanukkah, Kwanzaa, and Christmas all in one month. She's not Jewish; neither is she Christian nor African American. What she is, if anything, is very political correct. I'm sure it's well intended—I get that—but this lovey-dovey tolerance dilutes the meaning of something very deep and meaningful. A Christanukah party?

Tolerance or acceptance is not the same as respect. You see, copying traditions from the people around me will not bring me the essence and depth of the celebration; instead it disparages it—all good intentions aside. Is that what we want? I happen to celebrate Christmas, so please do wish me a merry Christmas, and I so hope you'll have a happy Hanukkah! I would love to hear all about it, or why you celebrate Kwanzaa, and how this is important to you. And if you invite me to celebrate the end of Ramadan with you—in your house—I would be so very honored to eat *klaicha* with you. Coexist.

The tiny village in the desert of Jordan, where the Christian teacher learns from the imam. Me, learning from my Hindu neighbor. A table full of big shots. Doing life together with respect and an open mind. Coexist.

One of my journeys brought me to Qatar, a beautiful peninsula, bordered by Saudi Arabia and the Persian Gulf. Qatar has oil, skyscrapers, richness, busy-ness, humidity and Abdi. When I arrived at the airport I was tired and jet-lagged, and happy to see the tall taxi-driver, waving a sign with my name. In Abdi's old scratched and beat-up car (with serious sound system), I could hardly hear a word he said, because Bob Marley blasted through the speakers. Abdi told me he was from Eritrea (more than 1,100 miles from Qatar). His wife lived and worked in the Sudan (about 1,200 miles from Abdi), and I explained to him how I had just flown from the Netherlands (a little over three thousand miles away). In our introductions alone, we had covered half of the world. Abdi was a great storyteller and we talked about reggae, Jamaica (more than ten thousand miles away), our families, countries, traditions, and beliefs. From completely different worlds, Abdi, Marley, and I. We couldn't be more different. But talking to Abdi made me realize we are all looking for truth and love: we have similar desires, dreams, and questions. We weren't so different after all. Coexist.

In 2007 Amsterdam was a front-runner of sorts. And this may surprise you because I'm not talking drugs and the red-light district here (I know that's where your mind wandered). Our teeny-tiny country stood out in representing the most nationalities in any capital—177 to be exact! We now live in Los Angeles (Ruth) and Jerusalem (David), both serious megalopolises, with a rich medley of nationalities and god-believers. A Jew, a Sikh, an atheist, a Muslim, a Christian, a Mormon, a Buddhist, a New Ager, and an agnostic, all under the same sun. The differences between us can easily lead to prejudice and pedantry in our worlds, in big cities, at work, and even in a small cab. If Abdi and I had focused on our differences, I probably wouldn't have made it to the hotel. Instead we had a lovely afternoon—showing each other our worlds, learning about our differences, looking at our similarities and what makes us tick. And for the differences? Wonder, respect, and an open mind. Coexist.

GOD OR NO GOD
That's the question

A man can live three weeks without food, three days without water, and three minutes without air, but he cannot live three seconds without hope.
—Lewis Mumford[9]

I'm not sure how one can measure hope, but I do take Mr. Mumford's word for it. Life without hope is pretty sad. We all hope. Maybe it's for a job, a new car, a long and happy life. A good report at the doctor's, for the woman with cancer. A father who won't drink tonight, for the abused girl. Tickets to Coachella, for the college student. To die in his sleep for the ninety-eight-year-old man with a pulmonary embolism, and an easy labor for the pregnant woman. Just imagine, no hope...absolutely nothing. Would life be worth living? Or would it leave us desperate and miserable, as Mumford says?

I would lose my mind without hope. While I'm too much of a coward to jump of a building, I would crawl back in bed, overwhelmed and deeply depressed. I've

---

[9] Lewis Mumford was an American historian, sociologist and philosopher (1895 – 1990). He wrote this in The Conduct of Life (1951).

never found life to be easy. Not that I have experienced real hunger nor been in real danger, and I am healthy and have not lost any close loved ones. A pretty easy life, when I compare my life to that of many others. Yet I find it a whole lot of moaning and groaning, life. A series of events, mostly out of my control. You don't have to have lived for a long time to realize this. A baby in her first months—and when lucky—will get everything she needs: food, warmth, comfort. But after a while her parents might let her cry at night. Or she might have cramps, maybe a cold. When she's four and learning how to ride a bike, she might fall and break an arm, and when she's sixteen chances are that she will be brokenhearted because her first boyfriend left her. There's just no escape. Life is not easy, and we are not in control.

I lived in Grozny, the capital of the Chechen Republic in Russia. It was horrid. Bitter cold, gray, and bare, and the sun didn't even bother to come out anymore. Everything was in ruins because of the war. I'd not seen so much sorrow and hopelessness ever before. The humanitarian aid organization I worked with set up camp in a container, and we did the best we could under the circumstances to bring some relief to the people. We also worked with children with post-traumatic stress. It was heartbreaking and difficult to imagine that we could make a difference. There were no schools, the economy was corrupt or nonexistent, and too many children were orphaned with nothing left. Anna, our translator, invited us to her mother's house. We didn't know what to expect when she brought us to the building, or at least what was left of it. The structure, just like the rest of the city, had been under heavy fire. Hardly any windows were left, and the walls (if they were still standing) were blasted with holes from the shootings. When we came closer, I saw a dot of yellow at the fourth floor and a little bit of blue. Curious we walked faster, what could this be in the midst of all gray? We climbed the stairs, curious while passing a large hole in the wall, and there it was… Clean clothes brazenly blowing in the wind! Hope! And Anna's mom, inviting us with open arms. She brought us to her kitchen table, which displayed everything she could find in her pantry. Nothing much, measured by my Western standards, but a feast here in Grozny. She held my hands and said: "Thank your parents for allowing you to be here. Now we know we're not forgotten!" Hope.

Solomon of Suleiman was king of the Middle East, and his story is recorded in the Talmud, the Bible, and the Koran. He's known as the wisest king and reigned over Israel through her golden years. Just for the record and to give you an idea of his wisdom, here's a little enumeration: he wrote thousands of songs and poems, had chambers and chambers full of gold, and had seven hundred wives (all royal blood), and three hundred concubines (commoners). Calculated by today's standards he made a little less than a billion per year (yes, with a *B*), and people came from far and wide to gape at his glory. For glorious he was. The story goes that God, in a dream, told him he could get anything he asked for. Carte blanche: riches, beauty, a long life, you name it. Solomon, the young king, asked for wisdom instead. "Give me wisdom and knowledge, that I may lead this people."[10] This pleased God, and God said: "Wisdom and knowledge will be given you. And I will also give you wealth, possessions and honor, such as no king who was before you ever had and none after you will have."[11] And so it happened. He became super rich. And super-duper

---

[10] 2 Chronicles 1:10 NIV
[11] 2 Chronicles 1:12. NIV

smart. And handsome too, I guess (with all the wives).

Solomon wrote three books. The first one he wrote as a young man, when he had just become king: Song of Songs. It's about love. Love and lust.

Then, when he was about thirty or forty, he wrote his second book. Proverbs is a collection of over three thousand words of wisdom from Solomon & Co. Three thousand of the wisest lessons, handpicked by Solomon! And his friends were not your average Joes with the latest Pinterest feel-good quotes, No, these were the most influential people and the highest scholars of his time. Proverbs—it's a good read.

His final book is Ecclesiastes. He wrote this at the end of his life, and if you ask me, he was dead tired and exhausted from ruling a country and those one thousand women. You could say that Ecclesiastes is a man's conclusion when he looks back on his life. He's a man who had everything that you can dream of, and despite it all, it's not a happy conclusion. Right in the first chapter Solomon writes: "In my opinion nothing lasts, everything is meaningless. What do we gain by laboring under the sun? Generations may come and go, but nothing really changes. The sun comes up, the sun goes down—All things are full of weariness beyond uttering."[12] He continues and says he tried it all. Laughter and merriment—meaningless. Wine, lots of *vino*—didn't change a thing. On to bigger projects, building houses, vineyards, and parks—*nada*. As well as slaves and servants—nothing. Silver and gold—*nyet*. Women—exhausting.

In short, he tried it all, had the power and the resources to do it all, and his conclusion was he hated it

---

[12] Ecclesiastes 1:2–5, 8. NIV

all. "So I hated life, because the work that is done under the sun was grievous to me. All of it is meaningless, a chasing after the wind."[13]

So much for optimism. Can you imagine the president addressing us like this in his State of the Union? "People, I did some pondering and reflecting, but life is just really tiresome, and completely hopeless. Utterly pointless. I wish you all the best, keep up the good work, and God bless America." (And the crowd cheered on...)

Dust in the wind, sings Kansas, all we are is dust in the wind[14], and we are just a drop of water in an endless sea. More happy thoughts. They continue by saying not to hang on. It all slips away anyway and nothing lasts forever but the earth and the sky.

In life there are no certainties, except for the sun; the sun will come up, and the sun will go down. "Under the sun" is an important credo in Solomon's books. It is really his thing, his mantra perhaps, and especially in Ecclesiastes it's mentioned a lot, twenty-nine times to be exact. With words, he draws a picture of everything under the sun. Literally. Life, you, me, the earth, and the sun. And everything in between he calls "under the sun." It's nothing but a chasing of dreams, and pretty much pointless, according to Solomon. Is this man a pessimist or what? A fool, a cynic? Or a realist?

Halfway in the book his perspective shifts, from "under the sun," to "over the sun," the things we cannot see. Fast-forward to today. In Solomon's time and in all his wisdom it was unthinkable that we would discover over one hundred billion galaxies. I can't even wrap my head around one, let alone one hundred billion. George

---

13 Ecclesiastes 2:17 NIV.
14 *Dust in The Wind*, by Kansas, 1977

Smoot, an astrophysicist and Noble Prize winner explains this really well in his TED talk "The Design of the Universe."[15] Look it up. You'll be amazed by the complexity and the systematic nature of it all, over the sun.

So, there you have it, says the wisest man who ever lived. To live a life under the sun will be disappointing, fleeting, and meaningless. Your life, my life—it's just dust. Not worth living, according to Lewis Mumford, for a life without hope is unbearable. Solomon didn't stop there, but concludes with hope! Something larger than life, beyond us. He says that there's hope when you look further, over the sun.

If your life is anything like mine, your time is swamped by things under the sun. The daily busy-ness. My skillset and talents, my money, and my energy are all putting it together for the demands "under the sun." There's nothing wrong with that. I work hard; I live well. But I can't help going back to Solomon's teaching. What if it's true? What if there's more than just "under the sun"? What if there isn't?

It basically leaves me with two options:

I can either live my life, strive for happiness, and enjoy everything "under the sun." There will be ups and downs, with the possibility to find out there was more. But I'm not going to worry about that now, that's for later… Carpe diem for now.

Or I can make a mindful decision to explore if there's more than I can see. A quest for the things "over the sun."

---

15 TED Talk, George Smoot: The Design of The Universe

I am my choices

I CANNOT NOT CHOOSE. IF I DO NOT CHOOSE, THAT IS STILL A CHOICE.

-Jean Paul Sartre
French Philosopher (1905-1980)

Sartre says you cannot not choose. Not choosing is still a choice. It's part of that thing called life. No matter who you are, what you are, and how you came to be, there are choices. And the beauty of living in freedom means that you and I, my kids, my neighbor, the president, and the mailman are free to choose what we want. I'm not going to tell you what to choose! I'm just saying that you cannot not choose; Sartre was right.

That's what this book is about. The choices you can make.

And the things over the sun.

W O R D I S M .

words like *religion*, *faith* and *atheism* have become loaded over the years. Tainted almost.

To avoid any misunderstanding I rather use the word **'god-believer'** for the man or woman who believes in a god.

Or you might not believe in any god. That makes you a **'non-god believer'**.

GOD OR NO GOD?
Still the question

I think you should be serious about what you do,
because this is it.
This is the only life you've got.
—Philip Seymour Hoffman[16]

On February 2, 2014, Philip Seymour Hoffman died. Instead of picking up his children, he was found death in his bathroom, with a needle in his arm. Cause of death: accidental overdose. He was forty-six years old.

Hoffman was a skilled actor who could portray the meanest man or biggest idiot in such a way that you would still relate to him. It's no surprise he won an Oscar, a Golden Globe, and many other awards. He was respected and loved by fans, critics, and film lovers alike. He and his family lived in Greenwich Village, New York, a happening, highly coveted place to be. He had a beautiful family, of which he once said that he'd rather spend time with his children than act, for being with

---

16 Philip Seymour Hoffman was an American actor, director and producer (1966–2014).

them was the real deal. As far as the American dream goes, this was pretty much it. He had it all.

I never met Hoffman and do not claim to know his mind, but the thought of someone fighting a deep and lonely battle—that seems bigger than life—is heartbreaking. Aaron Sorkin, producer and Academy Award–winning writer and friend of Hoffman, said: "Phil Hoffman and I had two things in common. We were both fathers of young children, and we were both recovering drug addicts. He didn't die because he was partying too hard or because he was depressed—he died because he was an addict, because of heroin."[17] And that hits the nail on the head. See, the problem with heroin is that she is a shameless seducer. She lets you believe that she is your best friend, not any BFF but a true companion who will always be there for you. No more anxiety, loneliness, or pain. Or at least a well-deserved reward after your next midterms. A sweet promise to care for you forever, as long as you keep her close. It's really kind of perfect. Who wouldn't want that? A halt to the dragging voices inside, the feelings of never being good enough, and a way to fill the void.

However, in her seducing stage, one minor detail is left out. She forgot to mention the dependency, and how she eventually will reveal herself as a raging devouring companion, who—just as promised—will never leave you alone.

It was heroin for Hoffman, maybe porn for someone else. Or food. Alcohol could be it. Cutting, gaming, gambling, money, or power. Or, or, or...you fill in the blanks. Whatever it is, the "it" that promises to fill the bottomless pit for now.

---

[17] Aaron Sorkin in the article "Philip Seymour Hoffman's Death Saved 10 Lives," for *Time*, February 5, 2014

Whether you're a big shot or you feel that nobody notices you, no one gets away from this. Just look around you, read the biographies of the most influential people, or ask the man on the street. We all have a void to suppress. Is it love? The desire of being known? Loneliness, gratification, or just pain? It's hard to find one word for it, for it's the mother of all loneliness, pain, and darkness. Whether you're poor, rich, warm, cold, loved, loathed, famous, overlooked, pink, or blue, nobody is a stranger to this. You may blame it on your past, your partner, your job, your neighbor, your dad—anything really—but I believe it's just life itself. Living life comes with this infinite hole, the restlessness of the void.

We become aware of the void as we fill it.

-Antonio Porchia, Argentinian Poet (1855-1968)

The promise of heroin is false. You know this, right? We all do. Porn, drugs, alcohol, power, lust, money, or whatever your fill-in-the-blanks are will only give an instant feeling of satisfaction. Yet the void is so much stronger and louder than that instant, and it will leave you with a deeper void. I've not met one person who is not struggling with this. Including me.

I live in Calabasas, together with the Kardashians, Will Smith, Justin Bieber, and Ben. Last week I couldn't get to the store because Justin Bieber was there and with him a zillion paparazzi. No biggie, you kinda get used to it, so I left. Yesterday I tried again and went back to the bookstore. On my way out I saw Ben. I really tried not to see him, making sure I looked all busy and important while I hurried to my car. Ben sat on a bench, filthy, homeless, and he was pretty much the last person I wanted to talk to. I'd rather meet Justin and have a story to tell. But there was a nudge inside me to get out of my car and talk to Ben. Sigh! Do you get those nudges? A silent voice telling you what to do at the most inconvenient times? I ignore them often, but this time I paid attention, stepped out of my car, walked to Ben, and asked him if I could get him something from the store. He said that he was hungry and that it would be great. So I went and came back a few minutes later with a sandwich, an apple, and a bottle of water. We started talking. I asked him how long he had been on the street and where he would sleep tonight. To my surprise, Ben was very easy to talk to. He told me how he had traveled from the East Coast to the West, about a year ago. How he lost his job, his family, his house, his life, everything really, because of alcohol. Ben was smart, funny, and articulate, and once he had it all. And now he has lost it all. His addiction started young, and he has not been able to shake it off.

Philip Seymour Hoffman started to use heroin when he was a student. He was clean when he was twenty-three. The next twenty-three years he was sober, building up his life, his career, and his family. A good life—he seemed to have it all. Until about a year before his death, he picked up heroin again.

The void is bigger than us, it's larger than life. That's why it can only be filled with something larger than us. Something "over the sun."

The god-believer says: God. Any god. The Buddhist says: meditation. Draw closer to yourself and be mindful. Oprah says: love. More love, and especially for yourself. The Christian says: Jesus. He will give you peace that surpasses all understanding. The atheist says: science. Find reason, it's the only way to make sense of life. And the Hindu says: nirvana. Find ultimate enlightenment, for this is the only way.

WHAT IF?

Is there anybody out there?

I want to know how God created this world. I'm not interested in this or that phenomenon, in the spectrum of this or that element. I want to know His thoughts; the rest are details.
—Albert Einstein, theoretical physicist (1879–1955)[18]

You know how our sun is really a star? Scientists estimate there are about two hundred billion to four hundred billion—give or take[19]—stars. And one of each five stars could have an Earth-size planet orbiting around them, just like our sun. They also discovered forty billion (that's 40,000,000,000 with ten zeros) earthlike planets. (Are you still following me?) Erik Petigura—a graduate student in the astronomy department at UC Berkeley—has always been fascinated by planets around other suns. He states that there could easily be one hundred billion, so forget about the forty billion! Our own Milky Way is

---

[18] Albert Einstein was a German theoretical physicist (1879-1955). He developed the theory of relativity, which is one of the two pillars of modern physics.

[19] I always wonder how they come up with a number like that. How does one give or take a couple of billions?

pretty big, but there's an estimate that there are one hundred to two hundred billion other galaxies in the universe! This goes way over my head, because I really thought we were a big deal! Remember the book *Men Are from Mars, Women Are from Venus*[20]? It ain't so. Turns out we were all Martians once. Steven Benner, a chemist, contends that life on our planet had to start somewhere else, and most likely on Mars. According to some, Mars once was a habitable place, and Earth wasn't. It all had to do with molybdenum, an essential enzyme for our human bodies, that was only found on Mars some billion years ago and not on Earth. So, men are from Mars, and women too. Now you know. The Russian Soviet pilot and cosmonaut Yuri Gagarin was the first human to journey into outer space. This was back in 1961. When he returned to Earth, safe and sound, he said: "I looked and looked and looked, but I didn't see[21]." My friend Hugh Ross, astrophysicist and author, says in his book *Why the Universe Is the Way It Is:* "If the universe were any smaller or larger, younger or older, brighter or darker, more or less efficient as a radiator, and if human observers were located where most stars and planets reside, the view would be so blocked as to give few (if any) clues about what lies beyond."[22]

---

[20] John Gray, *Men Are from Mars, Women Are from Venus* (United States: HarperCollins, 1992).

[21] It has been disputed if Gagarin said this and it might appear as he did, because Nikita Khrushchev said in a speech for an anti-religion campaign: "Gagarin flew into space, but didn't see any god there." Whether these are Gagarin's words or not, it think it is important to include, because most of us have thought this at one time or another- on the moon or in our own world. So my excuses to Mr. G if I have put any words in his mouth.

[22] Hugh Ross, *Why The Universe Is The Way It Is* (Grand Rapids: Baker books, 2008).

Is there anybody out there?

-**PINK FLOYD**
THE WALL

According to John M. Kovac, an American physicist and astronomer, we're really, really close to proving the Big Bang. His cosmology research focuses on observations of the cosmic microwave background. In other words, they used a serious telescope, literally at the end of the world—the South Pole—and measured waves so intense, generated in less than a billionth of a second (that's superfast). These waves can very well be the proof that our universe experienced a gigantic megaexplosion, a.k.a. the Big Bang. (He later withdraws his conclusion and said that they had altered the facts a little...)

Thus far are my scientific musings. Well, not mine, but from the people who know what they're talking about. My point is, that it's. Really, really B-I-G, and way over my head. But still we so badly want to know how we came to be and how it all started that we study and research for dear life, just to get a grip on things we don't understand. Proof of our existence! Robbert Dijkgraaf is a Dutch mathematical physicist and professor at Princeton. He notes that men understand less than 5 percent of the whole universe, and therefore will never be able to prove how the world came to be. In case you had your hopes up... Aristotle, the Greek philosopher and scientist, contests the notion that science can prove everything. He said: "The more you know, the more you know you don't know." Albert Einstein said: "I'm not interested in this or that phenomenon, in the spectrum of this or that element. I want to know God's thoughts; the rest are details." Socrates, another bright mind and Greek philosopher, said, "I know that I know nothing."

THE MORE YOU KNOW THE MORE YOU KNOW YOU DON'T KNOW

-ARISTOTLE, GREEK PHILOSOPHER (384-322 BC)

It was 2400 years ago that Aristotle and Socrates lived. In the last twenty-four centuries Einstein, Petigura, Benner, Gray, Ross, Kovac, Gagarin, and all mankind have discovered so much more. So many more answers. And many more questions too.

Can it be that there's no proof, that life and our existence remain one big mystery? No matter how smart we become, our findings will always be theories, beliefs? A combination of science, wonder, and faith? A belief, surpassing our intellect. An intelligent design? A wonderment?

Everyone believes in something, god or no god. The idea that we are coincidentally placed on a big sphere in the universe demands as much faith as the thought of a higher power designing it all.

It's time to look "over the sun."

MY AND MY THOUGHTS ARE WAYS ARE NOTHING LIKE YOUR FAR THOUGHTS, SAYS THE BEYOND LORD ANYTHING YOU COULD IMAGINE.

-ISAIAH 55:8 NLT

DOES GOD EXIST?
Yes / No

Is God Dead?
—*TIME magazine*[23]

As mentioned earlier, Kluun, a Dutch author and journalist, wrote a book claiming that God's a fool.[24] I like the book. It's a quick read, and if you want to unleash your inner Dutch, you should read it too. Kluun takes the reader on a journey to find out what well-opinionated Dutch men and women think of God. He not only asks the god-believers some key questions but also interviews scientists, atheists, Christians, Buddhists, celebrities, philosophers, journalists, and many more. He had three questions.

---

[23] "Is God Dead?" was the cover-story for the TIME magazine in April 1966. It hints to the famed phrase from Friedrich Nietzsche "Gott is tot" which is German for God is dead (1882).

[24] Kluun, *God Is Gek* (Amsterdam: Podium Amsterdam, 2010).

THREE QUESTIONS

Does God exist?
If yes, or if no, are you sure?
Is there life after death?

The interviewees had one thing in common. Just one. They were all human, and that was about it. They couldn't agree on the first question, if God exists. A few weren't sure. Most thought it to be ridiculous—the idea of a higher power—and a small group firmly believed in a god.

Nothing new under the sun. Just look around you, in your own group of people, your own tribe. I'm sure the answers are as diverse as this Dutch group. It's kind of a tricky question too. After all it's a *belief*. There's no proof, or it wouldn't be a belief. It's a strong sense for you— very personal, something that cannot simply be passed on.

Religion, yes. That you can pass on from one to another. My grandfather is Muslim or Christian, and so am I. Born into it. Inherited faith. But, as mentioned earlier, we're not talking religion here. We're talking *belief*. Or as the dictionary tells us: "a firmly held conviction that something is true." A strong conviction, a faith that determines who you are or what you're going to be. It would be pretty much worthless if you just take it from someone else or force it on someone else. It should be an opinion formed by your very own experiences, decisions and personality. It's all you.

But what are you? A *god-believer*, or a *non-god believer?*

Or, since life can seldom be brought back to one question, there's another option. You are in the middle. "Live and let live" is your motto. No need to deal with this now. You're young and you've got time, right? At least that's what it feels like. But there it goes, days become months, months turn into years, and all of the sudden life has passed by, without ever taking the time to really think it through…The daily hustle won. Or work. Or a game, a girlfriend, homework, a career, friends, or your followers on Instagram.

I think the quest for the existence of a god, or nonexistence of god, is a big deal. The answer to your personal quest will fill the void, and defines who you are, what you do, and who you'll become.

So why wait?

And if the whole god-thing is not such a big deal, why does everyone uses god's name? To pray, to curse, to joke, or as a simple exclamation. I haven't heard "Dear Caesar" or "Oh my Zeus" lately, you? Almost daily I hear: *Oh my God,*[25] *God damn it,*[26] *God bless America,*[27] *God forbid,*[28] *for God's sake,*[29] *Jesus,*[30] and *Godspeed.*[31] Just to name a few.

---

[25] "OMG, Baby!" —probably the most used filler word of this time. (Could be a good title for a book…)

[26] You're literally asking God to be damned…As in real suffering and condemnation.

[27] Sometimes used sincerely and other times used as an empty phrase.

[28] "I hope not!" is what we're really trying to say.

[29] To emphasize the importance of a situation.

[30] After you just hit your thumb with a hammer.

[31] Prosperity and good tidings to you.

Major Bosshardt

Everybody has heard of the red-light district in Amsterdam, aka de Wallen. But have you heard of Major Bosshardt? Probably not. She was a sweet older lady who worked in the red-light district. I say was, because se died in 2007, but she was well-known in the Netherlands- a real hero actually, although she would never accept the title. She worked with the Salvation Army and was known for her warmth, her directness, and her cups of hot soup that she gave to the homeless and prostitutes. And to anyone else who was hungry. She was kind of like our own Mother Teresa. I heard her speak one time in Amsterdam, and she told us the story of how she heard someone screaming one night, on her way home...

"HELP, God, help me! Help!"

She looked down in the canals, and sure enough there was a man in the water, nearly drowning and screaming for dear life. He obviously couldn't swim. She hurried down and helped him out. She gave him a blanket and of course a cup of soup...

"What happened?" she asked.

Shivering and upset, the man told his story. How he visited a prostitute, and after she did what prostitutes do, he got in a fight. He didn't like her service so refused to pay. Her pimp was close by and showed no mercy, but threw him in the cold water. He was so upset and thought it was so unfair how he was treated, and hoped Major Bosshardt would side with him. She looked him up and down, and he looked at her hopefully, this tiny, fine Christian lady. Instead she gave him an earful, how he should be ashamed of himself, and should apologize and pay immediately...

And the point of the story is?

When Major Bosshardt told the story she told us that she is convinced there will be a point in everyone's life that we will call out to God. Whether you are a god-believer or non-god believer there will be a moment for each one of us, where we seek His help.

Let's begin our journey. The quest for God, or no god. It may sound like a huge undertaking, but don't you worry—I've got a brilliant idea. A shortcut. We Are Going To Interview God! I think this is so smart, because we will have all the answers in one chapter. It will save me a lot of writing, and it will save you a whole lot of reading—four pages, max., to solve the world's biggest questions and some.

And these are the questions we will ask God:

THE QUESTIONS

Does God exist?
Is there life after death?
Who am I, according to God, or according to this philosphy?
What's the meaning of life?
How can I reach God (if He exists)?

With a case full of research and a healthy dose of imagination, we go.

God or

Upper-

When we talk about a *god*, you just say *god*—**lowercase**. It is a common noun. If you mean a more specific *god*, you use *God* —**uppercase**, as a first name, where the common noun becomes a proper noun, and uppercase is more appropriate. (Remember how your teacher once told you that if city is a common noun, then Tokyo and New York are proper nouns—it's the same with *god* and *God*. The only confusing part is when a *god* is actually called *God* and not another name, as in the city example.)

god
or lowercase

When referencing *God* or any other *god* the pronouns referring to Him are often capitalized as well.

For example: On their quest to a *god*, Sophie found *God*, but John didn't believe in Him and couldn't choose a *god* among the *gods*.

(You follow?)

INTERVIEW WITH GOD
A.k.a. the interview of the century

I am who I am.
—*God*

Me: God, do you exist?

God: Yes, I am who I am.[32] I am the beginning and the end.[33] And I'm the creator of everything you see,[34] and I am everything you see.[35] I'm also the highest being there is.[36] I'm not Kanye West, and Kanye is definitely not me.[37]

---

[32] God's answer to Moses when Moses asked who He was (Exodus 3:14).

[33] "I am the Alpha and the Omega…the Beginning and the End" (Revelation 22:13 NLT).

[34] Theists believe in one or more gods. They believe that the god (or gods) created the universe and holds it in His (or Their) hands.

[35] Pantheists believe that the universe *is* divine; the universe is god. Therefore the god (or the gods) manifests Himself (or Themselves) through everyone and everything.

[36] Deism refers to a supreme being for everything divine. In Hinduism, the supreme being is Shiva, in Islam Allah. In Judaism it is Yahweh or G-d, and in Christianity it's God.

[37] In the song "I Am God" by Kanye West, West refers to himself that he can be anything he wants to be.

Me: Yes, I had a feeling…But let's start at the beginning. How did You come to be? (Sorry, can't help myself, I'm already drifting away from the questions we agreed upon. I promise I will get back to it, but first a little detour…) Where You born a god?

God: No, I have always been. I'm the beginning, remember? The very, very beginning. And I will always be. It never ends. I'm also omnipresent. That means I'm everywhere, always.

Me: I don't get that. OK. The beginning—I'm really trying here. But what was first—before the beginning? It had to start somewhere, right?

God: It's like a circle. No beginning, no end. That's a way to grasp it.

Me: Is there a life after death?

God: Oh yes, absolutely. This is only the beginning. There are a few options. You've probably heard of nirvana? It means literally "blown out." Like a candle. It's perfect and the ultimate place to be. But first you'll come back here to earth as a better version of who you are now. This is what we call reincarnation, or rebirth. Eventually you will reach nirvana, a transcendent state in which you'll be free from the cycle of rebirth and death and free of karma. No desires, pain, or even a sense of self. Peace at last![38] Heaven is another option. People always ask me where heaven is, and I won't tell you its location, but trust me when I say it's a completely

---

[38] Buddhism and Hinduism.

different world. There's no pain. No suffering. You'll even have a new body and everything will be different. It's so amazingly beautiful![39] And of course there's hell. This place is deep agony. Hell is where I am not, so I won't be there with you, and I can't take care of you. And that's why it's so dark and evil. It's the opposite of everything happy, covetable, and beautiful. I have a question for you…Does darkness exist?

Me: Yes, of course. At night it's dark.

God: OK, true, nights are dark. But darkness in itself doesn't exist. We can experience darkness, just as you said, but only as an absence of light. And that's what hell is. An absence of Me. Everything that brings light can't be there. It's miserable and dark.[40] But don't worry. There's yet another option. What about no hell, at least not literally? More like a combination of all the bad things you've done. So, the more good you do, the more you love, the better your heaven will be. It's up to you.[41] Or, another possibility is that you won't die. There will be a period of rest. Soul rest. And I just wait until everyone has "died," and then there's the moment of judgment. Depending on your acts it will be heaven or hell. And if you're borderline good, you will enter a temporary hell, a purifying fire. And after this period of cleansing, heaven awaits.[42]

Me: Wow, that's really complicated!

---

[39] Christianity.
[40] Christianity.
[41] Judaism.
[42] Islam.

God: (smiling) Yes, it is. It's really up to you. Which brings Me to the next question: Who are you, according to Me?

Me: Wait, I'm the one with the questions! And how did You know what my next question was going to be?

God: I am God, remember? I know everything—we've talked about this.

Me: OK, whatever. How do you see us?

God: The journey of men is difficult and life is hard, but there's a source of wisdom and peace in one's soul, which gives a limitless strength. You will find this in meditation, mindfulness. It's a choice; it's not really me, because I don't really exist, I am the divine in each one of you.[43] But I do exist, I'm the only One! And I love people, each one of you. I created you. Even though I am God, I would love to be closer to you, have a relationship with you[44]. I gave everything to draw near to people.[45] But don't forget, I am God, and if you're mindful enough, you might draw near to Me[46].

Me: (more than a tiny bit frustrated...) That's three different things! I can find "it" in myself, You've already taken care of "it," or I might have a chance to get "it" if I work really, really hard...Can't you see why we are all confused? I just don't get it!
What's it going to be?

---

[43] Buddhism.
[44] Judaism, Christianity and Islam.
[45] Christianity.
[46] Hinduism

And that was it, my interview with 'god'. I gave up, waved goodbye and left.

I'm so lost.

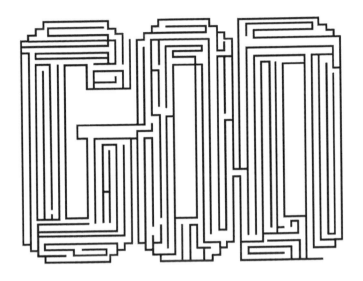

Lost in the God-Maze.

DIG DEEP(ER)
The world's greatest beliefs

God has no religion.
—Mahatma Gandhi, political Indian leader (1869–
1948)[47]

Well, that wasn't helpful at all, my little interview with God. It brought me exactly *nothing!* If anything, it confused me even more and showed me that we can't put God in a box. The god of the Muslims seems to be the same god as the god of the Jews and the Christians, but has different ideas. And the atheists have no god at all, Buddhism says god is in me, and Paulo Coelho tells us God has a thousand names. Really, Mr. C? That's it? After *The Alchemist,* you became quite an authority on all things spiritual for me, and now you tell me God has a thousand names.

---

[47] Mahatma Gandhi (1869-1948) was a political Indian leader, who led India's independence movement in the 1930s and 1940s from British rule with a non-violent approach.

God is the same, even though He has a thousand names;

it is up to us to select a name for Him

—PAULO COELHO,
By the River Piedra I Sat Down and Wept

What does that even mean? It sure is politically correct, but far too easy. Choose a name for your god, whatever feels good, whatever makes you happy, and you're done! Beautiful. Almost profound, until I really think about it. It doesn't mean a thing! Can I make my whole life depend on a feel-good solution that's made up by…me? And when it doesn't feel good anymore, I'll choose a new name for god, whatever works for that time? And with every name I pick, I choose attributes of what and how this imaginary god is. If it still doesn't work, I will change it again. And again. What's in a name, anyway? My personal boxed-in god. Put God in a box. Is that a god? Or a glorified idea of a god? Which is, basically, *an idea*. Nothing more, nothing less.

Hope is what we need. We did agree on that. Is this hope? Does it bring us some serious, sustainable, when-the-going-gets-though hope? Or is it a band-aid, just how people say: "it's going to be allright" when they don't know this for sure. When we rather have a moment of 'feel-good' than the truth. I call this fast-food hope. Eat three bags of chips, a large soda and a burger. Feels so good at the moment, but after the crash, you're exhausted and miserable. Fast-food hope.

We also talked about the importance of freedom, freedom to make our own decisions when it comes to a god. Is this the freedom we need? Build-a-god, and put him in a box. *I got the power!* But wait a second, if I get *this* much control, that I can design my own idea of a god, it doesn't mean a thing. If I have the power to create my own divine being, it will have as much divine power as I do, which is none. And you can quote me on that. I have no use for such a deity in my life. This divine being of mine is nothing more than an imaginary friend, an idea, that brings no substance, no hope.

If I have the power to create my own god, it will have as much divine powers as I do.

Which is none.

-SCHLEPPI-VERBOOM

To give Coelho the benefit of the doubt, I'd like to think that he isn't talking about a self-made deity but instead is trying to find a way to unite all faith groups, spiritual paths, and ethical systems—god-believers or not. I can appreciate that. I like that, after all, around the world there are about 4,200 of them. Yep, four thousand two hundred.

The good news is, for both of us, we're not going to talk about all 4,200 of them, because most of these groups happen to be related. If you look at their "family tree"—for the visual thinkers among us—you'll see there are five core groups: Judaism, Christianity, Islam, Hinduism, and Buddhism. These are the Don Corleone's of faith, the god-fathers (no pun intended). There are some similarities and nuances, but these groups are the main roots for all subgroups, and none of their gods is the same. *No kidding!* That's why I got stuck in my interview with God; I had all these gods in mind when I looked for answers, as if it was one god. It's kind of like creating my own god, as Coelho proposes, without letting the gods speak for themselves. It didn't work.

Forget the whole interview, our quest for god (or no god) begets a different approach. This time we'll let the gods speak for themselves and give them all their own chapter.

Remember how the Buddha is all for digging deep, six feet all the way? And I'm the "naysayer" who wants to explore first where to dig?

This is going to be it, the moment of the one-foot holes. In the following chapters, you'll find the basic facts of the different faiths and philosophies. Enough to give you an idea of what they are about, enough for you to know where you want to dig deeper.

We'll ask them the following questions:

THE QUESTIONS

Does God exist?
How did the world come to be?
Is there life after death?
Who am I, according to God, or according to this philosophy?
How can I reach God (if He exists)?
Tell me more! (a piece of history)

And before we start, one more note on the different religions: Our list wouldn't be complete if we didn't include atheism. And since it's the 21st century, we can't leave ietsism out. Ietsism is a new name for something that has been around for a long time. It's not just New Age, but way more. You'll see[48].

Here's a list of the religions and theories or philosophies we'll explore:

THE GOD-FATHERS OF FAITH

Hinduism
Islam   Judaism
Christianity
Atheism   Buddhism
ietsism

Let's go.

---

[48] On page 105, where it's all about ietsism.

HINDUISM
Brahma is it, and then some

You are not connected with anything. You are pure. What do you want to renounce? Dissolve this unreal connection and be one with Self.
—*Ashtavakra Gita 5.1*

I interviewed Shiva for Hinduism. Shiva is the third god in the Hindu triumvirate, a group of three of the most significant gods in Hinduism. Where other god-believers often worship a personal god, in Hinduism the gods are mostly impersonal. Except for Shiva. In many Hindu traditions, Shiva is the personal god. Therefore, an interview with Shiva.

Does God exist?

Yes, His name is Brahma. And within Brahma you'll find a trinity, consisting of three gods who are responsible for the creation, upkeep, and destruction of the world; Brahma is the creator of the universe, Vishnu is the preserver, and I am the destroyer of it, the transformer. Life is a continuous cycle in which destruction is needed to grow, to become. Besides

Brahma there are many other gods, all created by Brahma and as a reflection of Itself.

How did the world come to be?

The world and everything else is created by Brahma. It doesn't stop at Earth, but Brahma also created the universe and the spiritual and material world.

Is there a life after death?

Yes, although your body will perish. Your soul is carried into another body after you die. The essence of the soul remains, but your body will change. How it will change depends on how you lived. We call this *samsara*, meaning perpetual wandering. This is a continuous cycle in which the soul is reborn over and over again. Every cycle in samsara is different. You have the cycle of all things living in water, then all plants, reptiles, and insects are next, followed by birds; the fifth is the mammals and eventually human beings.

Who am I—what are humans—according to You?

Human life is characterized by suffering. It's the natural state of life. It's not useless, though, because through suffering you'll reach nirvana. As long as we are entangled in craving, we are bound in samsara, the continuous cycle. After a progression of insight, all earthly things will lessen and we will reach nirvana, the ultimate place of rest.

How can I get in touch with Brahma or the other gods?

God is in you, and God is everywhere. Do good, meditate, practice yoga, live mindfully, and you will draw nearer to God.

I'm definitely a practicing Hindu.

—JULIA ROBERTS, ACTRESS

Considerations like "I am this" or "I am not this"
are finished for the yogi who has gone silent realizing
"Everything is myself."

—ASHTAVAKRA GITA 18.9

Arjuna said: Of those devotees who worship you and those
who betake the impersonal absolute devoid and ultimate
Consciousness, who is most perfect in knowledge? Sri Krishna
answered: Those who are endowed with firm faith, beyond
material conceptions. Fixing the minds on Me, always engaged
exclusively worshipping Me.
They are considered by me the most superior of all.

—BHAGAVAD GITA 12.1-2

I'm a Muslim, a Hindu, a Christian, a Jew.
And so are all of you.

—MAHATMA GANDHI, INDIAN POLITICAL LEADER (1869-1948)

Certainly, never at any time did I not exist, nor you,
nor all these kings and certainly never shall we cease to
exist in the future.

—BHAGAVAD GITA 2.12

The strength I portray in the world of politics comes from
my experiences in the spiritual world.

—MAHATMA GANDHI, INDIAN POLITICAL LEADER (1869-1948)

The world is the wheel of God, turning around and round,
with all living creatures upon the wheel. The world is the river
of God, flowing from him and flowing back to him.

—THE SHVETASHVATARA UPANISHAD

Contrary to the common belief, Hinduism strictly speaking is
monotheistic. People worship one God in many forms, and Shiva
is one of the forms

—SWAMI TADATMANANDA, FOUNDER OF ARSHA BODHA CENTER

A piece of history.

More than any other god beliefs I find Hinduism the hardest to describe. Although it's the oldest religion in the world, there's not one way to explain Hinduism. For many it's more a way of life than a god belief, with deep connections to the Indian culture. Most Hindus can be found in India and Nepal. Hindus are polytheists, worshippers of more than one god—about 330 million to be exact. Brahma, however, is the most significant god. Brahma is not a personal god, but an entity consisting of three gods. First there's Brahma the creator, with four heads, which look out on the east, west, north, and south, and four hands, of which one is always raised to bless. Visha is the protector, and Shiva is the transformer or destroyer. Shiva has a third eye on Her forehead to ward off all evil. This third eye also symbolizes wisdom and power in the spiritual realms.

In Hinduism, nobody's limited to just body and soul. No, there's a god in your soul, the spirit. Everyone and everything has a god, and this god defines how or what we are. It's not always easy to experience this because life is full of distractions, but with yoga and meditation you will draw closer to your inner peace and rest. Imagine a dark room with a snake in it. Super dangerous and scary, but when we turn on the light, it turns out to be nothing more than a piece of rope. The light is our awareness. The more light you have, the more you'll experience and understand this godly world. On the other hand, the more you're involved in worldly stuff, the darker it gets, and you'll lose sight of the godly world.

And of course, there is karma, reincarnation, and the caste system.

Karma is the law of cause and effect. Your destiny depends on the way you live. Not just in this life, but also in past lives. You see, there's not only the afterlife, but there is the "before-life" too. Through reincarnation (*re* means "again" and *incarnation* means "becoming flesh") it will be better and better. That's why reincarnation is such an essential part of reaching our ultimate goal, nirvana. When we come to nirvana we're free from all suffering, castes, and karma. Free of reincarnation too.

The caste system is made up of four different groups. Brahma created these groups. The highest group is the Brahmans (these are the priests and scholars), followed by the Kshatriyas (rulers and warriors), and the Vaishyas (farmers and traders). The last and lowest group is the Shudras (workers and servants). And there's one more group who is casteless, meaning they are excluded from the fourfold *varna* system, and they are called the Dalits, the untouchables, or oppressed. An interesting fact about the Dalits is that Gandhi renamed them to Harijans—Children of God. A rebellious act, because the Dalits (about 150 million in India) are not supposed to be seen or heard. Gandhi was a big opponent of the caste system—not in its pristine state, but what men made of it. He protested against its hierarchy and suppression.

Hindus have several books, of which the Vedas is the most important and ancient. In the Vedas you'll find hymns, prayers, philosophy, and mythological formulas.

Hinduism is not an exclusive system, rather inclusive—accepting all religions as valid. Just like Mahatma Gandhi's famous words: "I'm a Muslim, a Hindu, a Christian, a Jew. And so are all of you."

BUDDHISM
It's in you, really

Do not accept my Dharma[49] merely out of respect for me, but analyze and check it the way a goldsmith analyzes gold, by rubbing, cutting and melting it.

—the Buddha

Here I begin an interview with the Buddha, the Enlightened One, on whose teaching Buddhism was founded. He is believed to have lived sometime between the sixth and fourth centuries BC, and some believe that he has never lived, but that the story and its teachings are the foundation of Buddhism. Regardless if he existed or not, I had a few questions for him.

Does God exist?

No. The idea of a god stems from fear. There's always a possibility of hunger, disease, death, or violence. These insecurities create fear, and to cope with this, we need a sense of control, so men created the idea of god. There's absolutely no scientific proof of god. And god as an

---

[49] Dharma in Buddhism are the teachings of the Buddha.

entity is unnecessary. Your god is with you. Buddhism helps you develop an infinite love, endless mercy, and understanding. It all comes from your own heart. By mindfulness we control the mind, and what the mind occupies, we will become.

How did the world come to be?

First of all, I don't think this question has any relevance in relation to ending human suffering. But I will answer your question regardless. We think in linear dimensions, with a beginning and an end. For example, the table you're sitting at, or this book—they are easy to grasp. However, there are countless other things with no beginning or end. Look at the sky above you. No beginning—no end. As it is with time. It all started with the destroying of the universe, which then evolved into the shape and form as we know it today. This took millions of years. From simple to supercomplex. All these transformations have no beginning nor end, but are again and again prompted by natural processes. To assume there's a god, and a beginning, is far too simple.

Is there a life after death?

Yes, death is not the end. It is the passing of our physical body, but our spirit remains and will find a new body and a new life. Our death is actually a rebirth. What, how, and where, all depends on karma and the way you lived. The cycle of death and rebirth ends in nirvana, the ultimate goal. Nirvana is freedom of everything. Free of pain, sorrow, perishing, and above all free from desire. It's unborn, unshaped, and non-existing—the opposite of the state you're in now: born, formed, being. You don't need to wait until death; nirvana can also be reached in life. Those who have achieved nirvana are called Buddhas, for they have entered Buddhahood. I reached nirvana when I was thirty-five.

Who am I, according to Buddhism?

Your main purpose in life is to end suffering. Men are under the constant pressure of human suffering, and life is frustrating and hurtful. This is because we seek fulfillment in things that won't give lasting peace. Even thoughts as "I have a self" or "I have no self" lead to suffering and stress. Enlightenment and awareness are needed to distance ourselves from this yoke of suffering. It is up to us, and if we can let go of our expectations, life is already more enjoyable. Eventually what we are is a result from our mind. The mind is everything; what you think, you will become. Peace comes from within—there's no use in looking for peace anywhere else. Your very self, just like anyone else in the universe, deserves your love and affection.

How can I become enlightened?

Enlightenment appears when fear ceases. Mindfulness helps to overcome our fears. Don't ever be anxious about what will become of you, and be independent of all. When you reject all help you are free. The path to enlightenment is meditation, and with this I mean the practice of consciousness and mindfulness. In Sanskrit, we call this *Shamata* or *Vipashyana,* a calming meditation.

One more thing about expectations: We become mindful if we intentional reject these thoughts. Not how it could be, but a deeper acceptance of how it is. Do not dwell in the past, do not dream of the future, but concentrate the mind on the present moment.

You take your problems to a god, but what you really need is for the god to take you to the inside of you.

TINA TURNER, SINGER AND SONGWRITER

Someone once asked the Buddha: What did you find in all your meditation? He answered: Nothing.
But I can tell you what I lost; anger, anxiety, depression, self-doubt, fear of aging and fear of death.

—ANONYMOUS

Only one thing I teach; suffering and the end of it.

—THE BUDDHA

If we learn to open our hearts, anyone, including the people who drive us crazy, can be our teacher.

—PEMA CHÖDRÖN, BUDDHIST TEACHER AND AUTHOR

Do not seek outside yourself, but turn the light inward; reverse the illumination and look within.
Be still, and meet your inner self.

—MAHATMA GANDHI, INDIAN POLITICAL LEADER (1869-1948)

Desire lies at the root of suffering.

—THE BUDDHA

The world is the wheel of God, turning around and round, with all living creatures upon the wheel. The world is the river of God, flowing from him and flowing back to him.

—PRAJNAPARAMITA

No one saves us but ourselves. No one can and no one may. We ourselves must walk the path.

—THE BUDDHA

Always follow the three R's. Respect for self. Respect for others. Responsibility for your actions.

—DALAI LAMA, HIS HOLINESS AND THE TIBETAN SPIRITUAL LEADER

A piece of history.

Siddhartha was born in the fifth or sixth century BC in what we now call Nepal. Born as a prince, and reared in Hindu culture, he was carefully shielded from everything miserable. His mother died in childbirth, and his father moved heaven and earth to give Siddhartha a carefree life, mainly by building large walls around the castle. He was married at sixteen, to a princess, and life seemed sweet. However, there was a deep longing and restlessness in Siddhartha for more, and one day (when he was twenty-nine), he sneaked out of the palace. For a man sheltered as Siddhartha and who was taught to believe that everything was (seemingly) perfect, this was a life-changing moment. Shocking. The streets were dirty, and for the very first time he encountered poverty. He met an elderly person, saw a sick man, and watched a body being cremated. What he saw that day created such an inner crisis that it would completely change his life. The idea that no one is free from suffering was unbearable for Siddhartha. He left his wife, his child, his wealth, and his whole princely being and embraced a sober and ascetic lifestyle.[50] He almost died after a few years of zealous fasting and discovered that this is not the answer to end suffering. After a bowl of rice and a warm bath, he realized that a life of moderation and balance works better. He meditated for a long time, and after a battle with the demon Mara he entered a state of enlightenment, nirvana. In other words, complete liberation. Siddhartha became the Buddha.

A Buddha is someone who has realized the enlightenment that ends the cycle of birth and death and

---

[50] An ascetic strives to live a life of severe self-discipline to reach a higher goal, by abstaining from any form of indulgence—such as comfort, food, sex, and/or relationships.

brings liberation from suffering. In Sanskrit *Buddha* means "awakened one." Everyone can become a Buddha, but only Siddhartha is *the* Buddha.

The Tripitaka is the holy book of Buddhism and entails the teaching of the Buddha. Some Buddhists believe that Buddha indeed lived seven thousand years ago; others say it is a saga, told from one generation to another. But whether he existed or not doesn't really matter since the Dharma is based on the teachings, not the teacher. Either way, Buddha's story is the foundation for Buddhism.

JUDAISM
There is only one G-d

*I am the Lord your G-d, and you will serve no
other gods.*
—the first two commandments in the Torah

Now I will interview Moses, one of the most significant
prophets in Judaism. *YHWH*[51], the god of Judaism, told
Moses to free the Jews from Egypt and bring them to
the Promised Land. Moses wrote the Torah, the main
book in the Judaic tradition.

Does G-d exist?

Absolutely. There is only one god, *YHWH*. He is
omniscient (knows all), omnipresent (is everywhere), and
omnipotent (can do all). Almighty and eternal He is.

---

[51] Another name for *YHWH* is G-d, both written without the vowels, to
avoid the risk of erasing or defacing the Name. In casual conversation
some Jews will call God HaShem, which is Hebrew for "the Name".

How did the world come to be?

YHWH created the world. The word of G-d brought everything into being: heaven and earth, mountains and rivers, and every living thing. Within six days He shaped a world of order and beauty. I wrote about this in the Torah. It wasn't really me, I should say: *YHWH* spoke, and I wrote it down.

Is there a life after death?

Yes, it's a time I long for. The *Olam Ha-Ba*—the world to come. We will see our ancestors, Abraham, Isaac, and Jacob. There is no war, only peace—no hate, just love, and even the animals will live together. The wicked will not be there, their souls will be tormented by demons of their own creation.

How does YHWH see people?

YHWH loves them and wants a relationship with us. That's why He created us with a free will. Freedom to choose between good and evil, G-d or no-god. He showed His love to us very clearly when He brought us through the desert, forty long years. Again and again He showed His love. He sustains, He guides, and He knows. G-d told me: "I know you, I know your name." We need that, to be known. In the desert again and again people doubted *YHWH*'s love, looking elsewhere   a new god, a new leader. And every time He showed us there was mercy. That's why He created the law, Halakhah, to keep us safe and as a constant reminder of our relationship with *YHWH*.

How can I find YHWH?

You can't see *YHWH*; He is so holy, you would die! His holiness demands respect and fear. *YHWH* is also a good god, compassionate and righteous. His justice is tempered by His mercy. He promises to take care of you, to give you peace, if you keep His commandments: the Ten Commandments I mentioned before, and all *mitzvah* (rules) you'll find in the Torah. Study the Torah. Or ask *YHWH* to reveal Himself. He is a holy G-d, so you won't be able to see Him like you and I see each other, but He does answer. You'll see.

I sought to hear the voice of God and climbed the topmost steeple. But God declared:
Go down again—I dwell among the people.
—JOHN HENRY NEWMAN, SINGER

Who did this to us? Who created Jews so different than all others? Who allows the suffering to be this horrid, even today? God created us as we are.
It will be God, who will save us.
After we've endured this suffering—and when there are still a few left of us—we will no longer be cursed, but be an example instead.

—ANNE FRANK

You're my hiding place, you'll protect me,
and fill me with a song of deliverance.
—KING DAVID, ISRAEL'S SECOND KING C.1000 BC

The Lord is my strength and my defense, he has become my salvation. He is my God, and I will praise him, my father's God, and I will exalt him.
—THE SONG OF MOSES AND MIRIAM, EXODUS 15,2

Judaism is my life.
Everything I do is through the lens of Torah.
—MATISYAHU, AMERICAN HEBREW RAPPER

Be strong and courageous! Neither fear, nor be dismayed of them, for the Lord, your God He is the One Who goes with you. He will neither fail you, nor forsake you.
—MOSES TO ISRAEL, IN DEVARIM (DEUTERONOMY) 31,6

Blessed are You, L-rd our G-d, King of the universe, who has chosen us from among all the nations and given us His Torah.
Blessed are You, L-rd, who gives the Torah.
—PART OF THE ALIYAH, A BLESSING OF THE TORAH

A piece of history.

Judaism or Jewish history, starts with the covenant established between YHWH and Abraham, roughly four thousand years ago, in the Middle East. Abraham was almost one hundred years old when YHWH gave him and his wife Sarah a son. YHWH had promised that Abraham would be the father of a great nation. His offspring would be as many as the stars in the universe[52], and as numerous as there are grains of sand. YHWH also promised Abraham and his family their own land, the Promised Land. Many see this fulfilled in Israel's declaration of independence in 1948, shortly after World War II. Jews have been oppressed for as long as we can remember. First in Egypt (before Moses led them through the desert to Kanaan), followed by the Babylonians, the Romans, and—fast-forward—Hitler. The oppression caused the Jews to scatter all over the world, but since the establishing of Israel in 1948, many have returned to their Holy Land.

The Tanakh is the book of Judaism and has three sections: the Orah, which contains the five books written down by Moses, inspired by YHWH, the Nevi'im, which are the books of the prophets, and Ketuvim[53] the remaining writings. A great deal of these teachings can be found in the Bible, in the Old Testament. Judaism doesn't recognize the whole Bible, the book of the Christians. You see, in the Old Testament, God has promised a savior. The Mashiach. Christians believe that

---

[52] There are a gazillion stars, as stated on page 41. The promise in itself is spectacular, but there's more to this. The promise was made when Abraham was seventy-five and Sarah sixty-five years old—beyond her childbearing years…Yet their son, Isaac was born when Abraham was one hundred and Sarah ninety years old.

[53] Ecclesiastes, the book by Solomon (Chapter 4—under and over the sun…) is part of the Ketuvim.

Jesus is their Messiah (or Mashiach) and the New Testament speaks of the life of Jesus. Judaism doesn't recognize Jesus as the Mashiach (or messiah), because there are several tasks that the Mashiach will fulfill. Jesus didn't fulfill these, and is therefore not the Mashiach. But more on Christianity in the next chapter, back to Judaism. Judasim believes the Mashiach, the promised One will be a great human leader, like King David. He will also bring political and spiritual redemption, by bringing Jewish people back to Israel[54]. He will establish a government in Israel that will be the center of all world government, both for Jews and gentiles[55]. He will rebuild the Temple and re-establish its worship[56] and the Mashiach will restore the religious court system of Israel and establish Jewish law as the law of the land[57].

---

[54] Isaiah 11:11-12
[55] Isaiah 2:2-4; 11:10
[56] Jeremiah 33:18
[57] Jeremiah 33:15

CHRISTIANITY
There is only one God, and Jesus is the way

"Are you tired? Worn out? Burned out on religion? Come to me···.Learn the unforced rhythms of grace. I won't lay anything heavy or ill-fitting on you. Keep company with me and you'll learn to live freely and lightly."
—*Jesus, in Matthew 11:28-30* MSG

An interview with Jesus, son of God. Jesus was born two thousand years ago in Bethlehem. He died when He was thirty-three years old—crucified, because He said that He was the Son of God, the promised savior. After three days, He rose from the dead. Christianity derives its name from Christ, Jesus Christ, and is centered around Jesus's death and resurrection.

Does God exist?

Yes, He does. God has always been; He is the beginning and the end. He is holy and a god of love. God is also a trinity, which means "three in one." He is God the Father, Jesus the Son (that's Me), and the Holy Spirit.

How did the world come to be?

There was nothing but utter darkness until God spoke. He said "Let there be light," and there was light. That's how He created heaven, the earth, and everything else. And He created people too, His masterpiece. First Adam, then Eve.

Is there a life after death?

Yes, there is heaven and hell. Heaven is beautiful: There is peace, and God is there. There is absolutely no pain and suffering. No sickness nor agony. Hell is the opposite. It's a horrible place, a place where God can't be. That's why it's so dark and horrid. There is pain, suffering, and the absence of peace.

How does God see people?

God created every one of you, to what He thought was the ultimate best version of you. Unique, with your own gifts, talents, and character. Blue eyes or brown eyes, curly hair or straight locks, introvert or extrovert, it's all hand-picked by the maker. God loves people so deeply and wants to be loved as well—but not with a robotic kind of love, which is why He gave you free will. It's your choice. God has a purpose for you: a purpose in life, and a purpose for eternity. Your eternal purpose is to be with God. This will make you whole. Many people think God is all about rules and guilt, but God is about grace and restoration.

How can I come closer to God?

Well, the relationship as it is, between men and God is broken, there is something standing between God and people. God is holy, almighty, and without any flaws. People are not; they make mistakes and are selfish. They try, but they mess up. This is called sin, and sin creates a gap between God and you. You can't take away your sin, no matter how hard you try. Good works might make you a nicer person, but it doesn't make you holy, and it doesn't take away your past sins. That's why God sent Me. 'For God loved the world so much that he gave his only Son, so that everyone who believes in Me shall not be lost, but should have eternal life. You must understand that God has not sent his Son into the world to pass sentence upon it, but to save it—through him. Any man who believes in me is not judged at all.'[58]

---

[58] according to John 3:16 (PHILLIPS)

This is how much God loved the world: He gave his Son, his one and only Son. And this is why: so that no one need be destroyed; by believing in him, anyone can have a whole and lasting life."

—JOHN 3:16 (MSG)

I believe in Christianity as I believe that the sun has risen: not only because I see it, but because by it, I see everything else.

—C.S. LEWIS, NOVELIST, ACADEMIC AND FORMER ATHEIST (1898-1963)

When people say, "Good teacher," "Prophet," "Really nice guy,"...this is not how Jesus thought of himself. So, you're left with a challenge in that, which is either Jesus was who He said He was, or a complete and utter nutcase.
You have to make a choice on that.

—BONO, SINGER, SONGWRITER, PHILANTHROPIST

"This man truly was the Son of God."

—ROMAN CENTURION, WITNESSING JESUS DIE ON A CROSS, MARK 15:39 (NLT)

This, in fact, is one of the main things that sets apart Christianity from all other world religions. All other religious systems essentially say Do: "Do this and you will have good karma, or you will get to Heaven, or paradise, or nirvana." In contrast, Jesus Christ says, "Done!" That's what it meant when He cried out on the cross, saying, "It is finished."

—GREG LAURIE, PASTOR

No one saves us but ourselves. No one can and no one may. I know men and I tell you that Jesus Christ is not a man. Superficial minds see a resemblance between Christ and the founders of empires. We've build our empires on power and strength. But Jesus Christ build his kingdom on love, and millions would give their life for this.

—NAPOLÉON BONAPARTE, FRENCH EMPEROR (1830-1893)

I am the way, the truth and the life,
No one can come to the Father except through me.

—JESUS, IN JOHN 14,6 (NLT)

A piece of history.

Christianity is based on Jesus, who is also called Christ[59]. The story however, started earlier, when God created the whole world and everything in it. God created people to have a relationship with Him. A real one, not robot-like, but by choice. That's why He created people with a free will. But the choices we make are often not good (the Bible calls this sin), and stand between God and us. God is holy, and we are not. That's why the relationship between God and people is broken. There is not much that we can do to restore this relationship. We can try by good deeds, being really nice and considerate, but all it does is make us a good person, it doesn't take away our sin. God gave us Jesus. His only Son. Jesus came as a human being to this world and was without sin- yet He took all the sin of everyone upon Him and paid the highest price. He died, so that we can come freely to God. It's the only way. If you accept Jesus, as your savior who died for your sins, there is nothing standing in the way between you and God.

Christians have the Bible; this is the Old Testament ánd the New Testament. The Old Testament consists of the storeis of how God created the world, of Israel, of how God wanted a relationship with people, and how people messed up, again and again. In the Old Testament you see how holy God is, how powerful, but also how merciful and forgiving. The New Testament starts with Jesus. How He was born by a virgin, how He lived, who His friends and followers were, and how He died, on a cross. It doesn't end there, because He rose from the death after three days. As a crescendo, kind of like Mozart's fifth. All this was prophesized (predicted) in the

---

[59] and Christians are the followers of Jesus.

Old Testament.

The rest of the New Testament is about the life of the first Christians, and the early church, and how they tried to live like Jesus. It also talks about heaven, and eternity, and that through Jesus people can be with God for eternity.

ISLAM
Allah is it, and Muhammad His prophet

*Worship the Gracious One, feed the hungry and
bring peace. And you will enter paradise in peace.*
—Muhammad

To learn about Islam I interviewed Muhammad, the
final messenger of Allah. He belongs to a long list of
prophets: Adam, Noah, Moses, Abraham, Jesus and
many others, but Muhammad was the most significant
one, to whom Allah gave his last revelation.

Does God exist?
Yes, there is only one god, Allah. He is the Creator,
omnipresent (He's everywhere), omniscient (knows
everything), and He is an everlasting spirit.

How did the world come to be?
Allah created the heavens, earth, and everything
within them in six days. And He created mankind, first
Adam, then Eve. It could have been six days, but for
Allah time is a different concept; it could very well have
been that one day was a thousand years.

Is there a life after death?

Yes, there's paradise and there's hell. Allah will decide where you'll go, depending on how you lived. It's like crossing a narrow bridge. You must cross the bridge to enter paradise, but under the bridge is hell. Those who are weighed down by their sins and actions during life will most likely fall from the bridge into hell—the consequence of their life's choices. But if you're not weighed down by sin, you will be able to cross the bridge and enter paradise. Hell has seven levels, each one more severe than the one before it. It's horrible, hell, not only physically but mentally too. Paradise, on the other hand, is wonderful. Delicious food, virgins, beautiful mansions, and nothing but physical and mental pleasure. Just as in hell, there are several layers in paradise, too[60].

How does Allah see people?

People are created by Allah and have a free will to choose between right or wrong, to choose to believe in Allah or not. Allah loves people and knows that life can be difficult. The difficulties in life are caused by the devil and his spirits (djinn). Allah allows this. For it will build your faith and humbleness. Your sins will be dismissed when you've proven to be faithful and humble.

How can I find Allah?

Surrender your life to Allah and to Muhammad, His prophet, and then you'll find Him. To surrender means you devote yourself to the five pillars in Islam: *Shahada, Salat, Zakat, Sawm,* and *Hajj. Shahada* is your faith in Allah. You must declare that there is no god but Allah

---

[60] There are some denominations within Islam who believe hell is a temporary state, and that after a certain time, you'll be purified, and Allah will receive you in paradise.

and Muhammad is His prophet. *Salat* is prayer. Five times a day, you send your prayers in the direction of Mecca. *Zakat* is alms, or giving to charity. You should give 2.5 percent of your income to Muslims in need, or to other religious purposes. *Sawm* is fasting during the month of Ramadan. And lastly *Hajj,* the pilgrimage. Every man and woman should try to make the trip to Mecca at least once in their lifetime.

Fear Allah, wherever you are. Follow up a bad deed with a good deed and it will blot it out.
And deal with people in a good manner.

—MUHAMMAD

Be peaceful, be courteous, obey the law, respect everyone;
but if someone puts his hand on you,
send him to the cemetery.

—MALCOLM X, AMERICAN MUSLIM MINISTER AND HUMAN RIGHTS ACTIVIST (1925–1965)

Declare your jihad [spiritual battle against sin, or battle again
non-believers] on thirteen enemies you cannot see—egoism,
arrogance, conceit, selfishness, greed, lust, intolerance, anger,
lying, cheating, gossiping, and slandering.
If you can master and destroy them, then you will be read to
fight the enemy you can see.

—ABU HAMID AL-GHAZALI

Except for those who repent, believe, and work righteous
deeds. For those, Allah will change their evil deeds into good
deeds, and Allah is Most Forgiving, Most Merciful.

—KORAN, SURAH 25:70

I challenge anyone to understand Islam, its spirit, and not to
love it. It is a beautiful religion of brotherhood and devotion.

—YANN MARTEL, LIFE OF PI

Verily, I am Allah: There is no god but I: So, serve thou Me
(only), and establish regular prayer for celebrating My praise.
Verily the hour is coming. My design is to keep it hidden for
every soul to receive its reward by the measure of its
endeavor.

—KORAN, SURAH 20:14–15

I did not come into contact with any Muslim before I embraced
Islam. I read the Qur'an first and realized no person is
perfect, Islam is perfect, and if we imitate the conduct of the
Holy Prophet...we will be successful.

—YUSUF ISLAM, FORMER KNOWN AS CAT STEVENS, BRITISH SINGER-SONGWRITER

Worship the All-Merciful, feed the hungry, and spread peace.
You shall then enter Paradise in peace.

—MUHAMMAD

A little bit of history.

Islam is a monotheistic faith, meaning there is only one God, just like Christianity and Judaism. There are several prophets, of which Muhammad is considered the greatest. He received revelations from Allah through the angel Gabriel, and was sent by Allah to guide humanity to the right way. His message was one of honesty and righteousness. This caused a lot of friction in Mecca, his hometown. You see, Mecca was the center of trade and merchants in those days, and the whole honesty thing wasn't good for business. Muhammad moved away from Mecca to Yahtrib (later named Medina), and all his followers came with him. A historic event for Muslims, this migration happened in the year of 622. It is the beginning of the Islamic lunar calendar. Muhammad was born in 570 and died in 632.

The holy book of Islam is the Koran, and Islam is the fastest-growing religion today (the second largest after Christianity). It is projected that they will leap from 1.6 billion to 2.76 billion by 2050. A good Muslim is the person who completely surrenders to Allah and His prophet Muhammad. This means living according to the five pillars of Islam, as mentioned before: *Shahada* or faith, *Salat* or prayer, *Zakat* or charity, *Sawm* or fasting, and lastly *Hajj*, the pilgrimage to Mecca.

A note on extremism.

Islam has gotten a bad rap lately, with ISIS, extremism, and terrorists. Donald Trump proposed a total ban on Muslims entering the United States during his presidential campaign. Trump said that the Islamic faith is rooted in hatred and violence. It can seem like that, but is not true. Many verses in the Koran speak of love and responsibility, and Muhammad has said,

"Kindness is a mark of faith, and whoever is not kind has no faith." Islam means literally "peace, submission, and obedience." The Koran does speak of hate and fierce revenge, too, just like the Bible, the Torah, the Vedas, and many other teachings. When we disagree on something, or even worse, when we feel threatened by it, we tend to take things wildly out of context. Extremists do this too and justify their actions by these verses. The terrorists in the news today all seem to be Muslims, but this doesn't mean that all Muslims are automatically terrorists or extremists. In chapter 2, "Faith ≠ Religion," we talked about angry Buddhists, ridiculous Christians, horrible Hindus, and a few more.

To use Rumi's words once again: "Silence is the language of god, all else is poor translation." Or…to use my very own words again: "I believe that if a god or deity needs me to fight its battles, it's not a god."

ATHEISM
God is definitely not it

All thinking men are atheists.
—*Ernest Hemingway*[61]

This interview is with Chris, my imaginary friend the atheist. Atheism has become a broad term for "no belief in God or gods." Just like many theisms (god beliefs), atheism stems from all kinds of different influences. We wouldn't do atheism justice if we fit it in one box or if we spoke to only one atheist. I'd rather give you Chris, a combination of all the atheists I've met in real life and on the web. Say hi to Chris.

Does God exist?

No, there's no god, and no higher power. I haven't found any evidence for Zeus, Allah, Jehovah, or any god. If there's a god, I would love to talk to him. But I never met him or it, and if he doesn't show up, you can't convince me of its existence. I need proof—facts and scientific proof. To all the theists (god-believers) out

---

61 Ernest Hemingway was an American journalist and writer (1899-1961)

there, the burden of proof is on you. Or if *you* can't proof it, it's on the god himself.

How did the world come to be?

Who knows? Nobody really knows. Although there's more and more evidence that our universe is the result of a cumulative occurrence of cosmic events. Evolution.

Is there a life after death?

You see, the reason for being is really our mind. It's the whole core of my existence. If I die and my mind ceases to be, so will I; there is no use for anything else. Don't kid yourself that you're going to live again after you're dead, because you're not. Or don't fool yourself that you will live on one way or another. Over the years we've made that up because we couldn't deal with reality. But it's not true. You should make the most of the life you've got. Live it to the full, because this is it.

Who am I—what are we people—according to atheism?

We are intellectual beings and have a responsibility to test and research everything according to the law of science. In my opinion a god is too easy of an answer. Take moral and ethical issues. You don't need a god to teach you those. It's a built-in essential for every human being. If everyone would live with empathy, listen to conscience, and follow the order of life, we would live well together. Theists believe that their gods morally guide them. The opposite is what I see! Many theists hate (they call it justice), look for revenge (they call it righteousness), or start a war (whatever they call it...). They play god, or at least their idea of a god.

Chris, my next question we might as well skip…it was: How can I reach God?

No, don't skip this question; turn it around! Ask yourself the question: How will god reach us? If there is a god, he should come to us. Why doesn't he show himself? According to my god-believing friends, it would be an easy thing to do for a god. But I haven't seen him, and the proof is up to him.

Whoever believes in God after Darwin, is a fool.

—Dr. Ronald Plasterk, Dutch politician, coined the term Ietsism

Faith is the great cop-out, the great excuse to evade the need to think and evaluate evidence. Faith is belief in spite of, even perhaps because of, the lack of evidence.

—Richard Dawkins, British ethologist, evolutionary biologist, and writer

The only position that leaves me with no cognitive dissonance is atheism. It is not a creed. Death is certain, replacing both the siren-song of Paradise and the dread of hell. Life on this earth, with all its mystery and beauty and pain, is then to be lived far more intensely: we stumble and get up, we are sad, confident, insecure, feel loneliness and joy and love. There is nothing more; but I want nothing more.

—Ayaan Hirsi Ali, Somali-born activist, author, and politician, in Infidel: My Life

God is not so much the object of our knowledge as the cause of our wonder.

—Kallistos Ware, English bishop within the Eastern Orthodox Church

If God doesn't exist, everything is permitted.

—Fyodor Dostoyevsky, Russian novelist, journalist, and philosopher

Nonsense! Ethics, empathy and reason have been linked to religious ideas and beliefs for far too long.

—Dirk Verhofstadt, Belgian social liberal theorist

My definition of God is humanity and the love of humanity. I don't belief in a god, but am in awe of nature, the ocean, and humanity.

—Diana Nyad, long-distance swimmer, with Oprah Winfrey on Super Soul Sunday

Trust is not the same as faith. A friend is someone you trust. Putting faith in anyone is a mistake.

—Christopher Hitchens, literary critic and journalist

A piece of history.

Atheism is an absence of belief in God, gods, or any higher powers. It literally means "without god." A = (without) + *theos* (theism, God) = without god. That's a super-broad definition, which gives freedom for all kinds of interpretations. There are many different movements within atheism, just as there are in theism. In theism, we classify them into different religions and beliefs, but it's different in atheism. That's why there's no conclusive number if you tried to count all the atheists around the world. Atheism is often mistaken for agnosticism or ietsism, which is something completely different. An agnostic is somebody who believes or doesn't believe in something. They have not ruled it out one way or the other. An ietsist believes there is something (more on ietsism in the next chapter); it's very much maybe and something. Atheists have ruled out faith in anything. George H. Smith explains in his book *Atheism: The Case against God* (1989) how there are two groups: implicit and explicit atheism. Implicit atheism means the absence of theistic belief without a conscious rejection of it.

You just don't believe it or have not considered it any further. Explicit atheists have thoroughly considered and researched all deities (or at least the idea of them) and don't believe that any deity exists. Since more and more people call themselves atheists, the hard-core atheists found the need to distinguish themselves from this group, so they founded New Atheism (in the early 2000s). Their criticism of other atheists is that they are too vague, just watching from the sideline. To which the implicit atheists responded that they are more tolerant to theists. New Atheism finds implicit atheism weak, and New Atheists distinguish themselves by taking an active role in politics and science. Christopher Hitchens said:

"What annoys me most is a lazy argument." Hitchens, Richard Dawkins, Sam Harris, and Daniel Dennett are some of the front-runners of New Atheism. They believe that a god-belief is not only untrue, but harms humankind more than it helps. Therefore religion should not simply be tolerated, but instead it should be countered, criticized, and exposed by rational argument.

These are the "official" groups in atheism, but personally I've found a third group. These are the people who turn down religion. British actress Emma Thompson described it so well, when she said in an interview: "I'm an atheist. I regard religion with fear and suspicion. It's not enough to say that I don't believe in God. I actually regard the system as distressing: I am offended by some of the things said in the Bible and the Koran, and I refute them."[62]

I believe this form of atheism is not atheism per se. It's antireligionism (if that could be a word) because it's having no faith in the system—the religion—turning down the religion and therefore its god. Religion has polarized and influenced culture, life, and politics around the world for many years, and at times this was a good thing. But religion has spoken loudly and oftentimes louder than its gods. As a reaction to this, people rather dismiss religion at all and make decisions on what they think is valuable, not the inherited religions. This is especially happening in the Western world. I get that, but the danger can be that we think we know the religion—because we've lived with the rules and regulations of it––yet we don't know its god or what it really is about. We throw out the baby with the bathwater, as they say.

---

[62] Thompson in an interview by Jane Cornwell for *The Australian*, on October 15, 2008

IETSISM

There is something, and it could very well be god

We have talked about atheists, Christians, Muslims,
Buddhists, Hindus, and Jews, but the list wouldn't be
complete if we missed one of the fastest-growing groups
in the land of the spiritually minded: Ietsism. Ietsism
represents the people who believe in "something," in *iets*.
Wikipedia says ietsism (pronounced [itsˈɪsmə])—
"somethingism"—is an unspecified belief in an
undetermined transcendent force. Now you know. Or
now you know nothing, because it's a description with
freedom for all to fill in what the something is. You are
probably more familiar with the term New Age. New
Age is a big part of ietsism, but ietsism covers more than
just New Age. New Agers are conscious seekers of
spirituality, of something higher. An ietsist can be an
active seeker, but does not have to be. Let's ask the ietsist
himself, because just as I can't explain to you what

'something' is in a few words, I can't explain ietsism through one person. So, let me introduce you to…Someone. Meet Someone. He's from all races, colors, genders, cultures, and mind-sets. Quite handsome too. And since ietsism is the fastest-growing group out there, you probably have one or more Someones in your life too. He or she could be your neighbor, your boss, your buddy, your mailman, or your daughter. Or what are the odds, it might even be you!

Does God exist?

Oh yes, there's definitely something. I am very spiritual, and there must be something, but I'm not sure if I would call it god.

How did the world come to be?

I'm not sure. It could be created, or it could be evolved, or more likely a combination of the two. Nobody knows exactly when and how. But there must be something—a higher power—that is in control.

Is there a life after death?

Again, I'm not sure, but I hope there is. It's a little hopeless without. Abrupt too. We die and there's nothing? I surely hope not. There must be something. But I'd rather talk about life, and how we are divine by nature, and how our ultimate purpose in life is to find our own goodness—that's the divinity within. In our journey to our own divine goodness we unite with men, nature, and with god.

How does Iets, or god sees people?

How do we see people? Good, people are good. But it's a lifelong journey to develop this goodness in us.

Some are more aware and are further in their journey of truth, acceptance, and the individual notion of reality itself. We have so much good in us. There must be goodness in people; it would be horrible without it.

How can I find It? God, or Iets?

It's intuition. The way you find *it* is different from mine. I think you can feel *it*; it's a gut feeling. Deep down, we have *it* in us and know what to do. But life and its distractions have cluttered our view, and we should strive to go back to our deepest self. *It's* still a higher power, so I'm not sure if we can reach *it* on the same level that I can be in touch with you, but a good start is to do good. Mindfulness. Live in the moment, and trust your gut. If we do good, we will see more and more of the truth.

God is the same,
even though He has a thousand names.
–Paulo Coelho, in By the River Piedra I Sat Down and Wept

I'm not sure, but I'm appealed to believe
in a transcendental power.

–Kluun, author, in God Is a Fool

There is a god for some people. I hope so, for them. For
the people who believe in it, I hope so. There doesn't need
to be a God for me. There's something in people that's
spiritual, that's godlike. I don't feel like doing things just
because people say things, but I also don't really know if it's
better to just not believe in anything, either.
–Angelina Jolie, actress, filmmaker, and humanitarian

Ietsism is, in my opinion, another word for searching.
–Marjolein de Vos, Dutch poet

I respect all religions, but I'm not a deeply religious person.
But I try and live life in the right way, respecting other
people. I wasn't brought up in a religious way, but I believe
there's something out there that looks after you.
–David Beckham, English former professional footballer

I would never die for my beliefs because I might be wrong.
–Bertrand Russell, philosopher, mathematician, writer, and political activist

Plasterk initially called ietsism: "An annoying sign of our time."
But later said he preferred ietsism over Theism: It's like
atheism with a whiff of nostalgia. Intellectually poor, but much
more sympathetic than the idea of some angry god, who wants
all this misery."
–Ronald Plasterk, author, molecular biologist, and Dutch politician

Still haven't found what I'm looking for.
–U2, from the album The Joshua Tree

A little bit of background on Ietsism.

Or how the Dutch invented a new belief...just kidding! Ietsism has always been there, and a Dutchman just happened to put a name to it. Ronald Plasterk, author, molecular biologist, and Dutch politician, was the first one to use the word *ietsism* to describe the spiritual opinion of people who say there's something bigger than us. These men and women have turned their backs on traditional beliefs and the church, but have not lost faith in spiritualism, or a god, or in something. Plasterk initially called ietsism: "An annoying sign of our time." But later said he preferred ietsism over theism.

Ietsism is an unspecified belief in an undetermined transcendent force. That's as specific as it gets.

And why haven't we heard of this before? Well, I think we have. You see, in the last decades more and more people grew dissatisfied, disappointed, or weary with the traditional beliefs. Many people lost faith in religion as an institution but did not automatically discharge the idea of a higher power or god. An ietsist can believe parts of the other beliefs, mix and match and combine, or create a whole new *iets*. Ietsism is a major umbrella term. Everything that doesn't fit in a specific religion or fall under atheism is pretty much Ietsism. If I could draw you a picture I would draw an umbrella with all kinds of ribbons attached to the ribs. On the ribbons would be the following words: agnosticism,[63]

---

[63] Where one believes it impossible to prove the existence of a god, but doesn't completely discard the possibility of it.

polytheism,[64] pantheism,[65] New Age,[66] Seeker, and many more.

And although I disagreed with Coelho in chapter 9 (Dig Deeper), I do believe he was on to something. When he wrote in *By the River Piedra I Sat Down and Wept* that there are "A thousand names for a god—" he described ietsism at its core. A broad, nonexclusive, open-minded interpretation of what fits you. A thousand names for your god.

I believe that Einstein was an ietsist—don't quote me on this, because I've never talked to the man, but he said: "I am a deeply religious nonbeliever. This is a somewhat new kind of religion." His conception of god was pantheistic, although he didn't call himself a pantheist or an atheist. He concluded that "the problem of God is too vast for our limited minds," and could not be answered "simply with a yes or no."

Marjolein de Vos, a poet and ietsist, says: "Ietsism is being in a spiritual pursuit, a quest." You're open and still growing, looking and not excluding anything.

OMG! I think that's us!

---

[64] One who believes in more than one god.

[65] The belief that the universe is the divinity, or that everything composes an all-encompassing, immanent god.

[66] New Age can be as broad as ietsism, but it is a collection of Eastern-influenced spiritual paths.

ME, MYSELF, AND I
What do you think?

Everyone has the freedom to choose,
continuously. We can only choose for ourselves,
not for others. Once we allow others to choose for
us, we fail ourselves, and our confidence in Self.
—Goos Geurtsen[67]

There you have it. The chapter on Ietsism concludes our digging of the one-foot wells. What do you think? After Moses, Shiva, the Buddha, Jesus, Chris, Muhammad, and Someone, it's your turn. After all, it's your decision to make. Sartre said it: I am my own choices, but I cannot not choose[68].

And to sum it all up, I've made little mind map.

---

[67] Goos Geurtsen was a theoretical physicist (1879-1955).d
[68] I am my choices. I cannot not choose. Even if I don't choose, it's still a choice. —Jean Paul Sartre

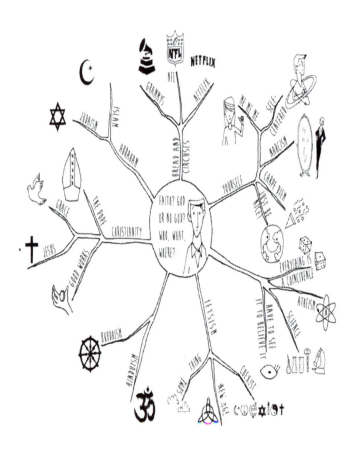

Does god exist?

....

....

How did the world come to be?

....

....

Is there life after death?

....

....

How does God see us? Or, if there's no god,
who are we, and why are we here?

....

....

Where can I find God (if there is a god)?

....

....

SUFFERING

If there's a god, why does He allow suffering?

Either God is responsible for the tsunami or God
is not in control.
—Rev. Tom Honey[69]

In preparation of this book, there was one question that stood out. In almost every conversation, Internet search, interview, YouTube video, or book about God or no god, the same question came up. You can put it in a million different words, but it's a question we all have. The question about suffering.

THE QUESTIONS WE ALL HAVE

If there is a God, why does He allow suffering?
If God is almighty, why doesn't He stop the misery?
With all the pain and hurt in the world,
where is God?

---

[69] Reverend Tom Honey gave a TED talk on "How Could God Have Allowed the Tsunami?"

To live
is
To suffer

to survive
is to find
meaning
in the
suffering.

Friedrich Nietzsce
German Phiosopher (1844-1900)

Whether we're talking gods or no gods, this is a question everyone has, and it would be ignorant to dismiss this.

I won't. But I can tell you right now, that there's no simple answer. Or worse, there might not be an answer at all. At least not an easy one.

In life, there's suffering and suffering, and just to make sure we're talking about the same thing, and not comparing apples with pears, we need to define the different kinds of suffering.

The first one, and I'm not going to sugarcoat this, is merely caused by our own stupidity. Dumb choices or an act of human fuckery, as Stephen King once put so lovelily in *The Stand.* Cause and effect, or the simple result of poor choices we made. If I don't study for my finals, I'll fail. If I keep falling for the wrong guys, I might end up in an abusive relationship. When junk food is all I eat, I'll be miserable and obese. If I drink and drive, I might get a DUI and lose my license. If I don't stop for a red light, I…well, I think you get the picture. We can cry, "Oh God, why me?" all we want, but it wasn't God who got us into the mess in the first place, it was basically us. I'm not trying to trivialize these situations; I know the choices we make have a deeper cause, but at the end of the day, it is what it is—an agonizing and ongoing process of our own human screwups.

And then there's the other kind of pain, caused by horrible choices of others. Not my fault and undeserved. "Why doesn't God protect me from these? Isn't He almighty and in charge?", we've all asked. Good one, I agree that we do not deserve this and some of the difficulties in life are so unfair! I wouldn't mind to play God in this. Or just help God. Kind of like being God's assistant. Imagine if we could do that… What if we could actually help God, and bring justice to an unfair world. Let's do it. Get out a marker and a big piece of paper. Draw a big circle. Everyone on the outside can go; everyone in the circle stays. I got this, God! This is easy. Let's start with the terrorists. I think we can all agree that they can go. Outside of the circle with them. Child molesters, rapists, and murderers, they can all go too! More and more names are outside of the circle. What about the thieves and frauds? Out! The hypocrites, the liars, and the bullies? The circle grows smaller and smaller, and it comes awfully close to me. The haters and the selfish ones? The gossipers and the lousy drivers? The jealous ones? The people who cut in line? The pessimists or the …? Where do we draw the line? If God would wipe all of them from the face of the earth, I would probably not survive either. The choices I've made have hurt other people, just as their choices have hurt me. There's really bad, kind of bad, and not so bad at all, but who will be the judge of that? There's pain either way.

The third kind of suffering is the suffering of innocent people. The tsunami, a tornado, famine, or the girl who got raped. The man losing his wife to lung cancer (when she'd never-ever smoked), the child molested by his parents. Horrible, sad, and unfair. This is the kind of suffering with no answers. And this is the kind of suffering that can make life so unbearable, when things happen outside of our control.

Glyzelle Palomar was only twelve when she met Pope

Francis. It was January 2015 when Pope Francis visited the Philippines, and thousands and thousands of people came out to see him. Glyzelle lives in a home for abandoned children in Manila. She was asked to say a few words to the pope, but in front of the large crowd, she had just one question. Timidly she asked the question we all have: "Why does God allow these things to happen to us[70]? The children are not guilty of anything." There he was, Pope Francis, sitting in all his glory, thousands of people before him, and this little girl Glyzelle looking him in the eyes. Listening to her, he was quietly and visibly moved. The pope had no answer. He simply stood up and hugged her. No words, only compassion. Pope Francis later told the press that her question barely had an answer. "Only when we're able to cry we're able to come close to responding to your question. Have I learned to weep, how to cry when I see a hungry child, a child on the street who uses drugs, a homeless child, an abandoned child, an abused child, a child that society uses as a slave?"[71] he added.

No answers, just listening with an open heart. What is there to say? Suffering and pain are so deeply personal. Others can be there for you, hold you, weep with you, but at the end of the day, it's your journey.

Suffering seems to be an inevitable part of life, everybody's life. And if I were you, this would be my first question to God, any god! Whether you believe in a god or not, whether you are an atheist, an ietsist, or a god-believer, ask Him! Do not rest until you get to the

---

[70] Referring to the children suffering through child abandonment and child-trafficking and prostitution.

[71] From an article by the Catholic News Agency: "What Pope Francis Learned From Homeless Girl", www.catholicnewsagency.com

bottom of this. Do not be afraid to yell, doubt, and kick with angry questions.

The courage to admit doubt is part of the soul's growth, and if your god can't deal with it, it's not a god to begin with.

How does your god, belief, or philosophy answer questions about suffering?

If I put my faith in a god, a belief, or philosophy, it's got to hold up to the bigger questions in life. It's worthless if it's not able to sustain me. And it's of absolutely no use to me, if I have to tread it on eggshells.

Very often nonbelievers start blaming God when the going gets tough. They've never believed in a god, and all of a sudden they blame God for their pain. Do you blame God? Tell Him! Are you exhausted, weary, and hurt? Don't hold back. Are you so frustrated and angry with all the injustice in this world? Disappointed? Broken? Anxious and paralyzed from pain and desperation? Shout it out! Be true to yourself, and honest with your god! What good can faith do if it can't give you a lasting peace and hold you in times of despair?

For how much worth is a god, if He can't handle your desperation, if He's afraid of your questions, and if He can't hold your pain?

I have a friend who wanted to take her life when she was seventeen. The only thing standing in her way was that she couldn't find anyone to help her. She wasn't able to do it herself because just weeks earlier she'd broken her neck. Paralyzed from the shoulders down, there were no hopeful prognoses and no cure—and for the rest of her life she would have to depend on others for everything! Eating, bathing, going places, scratching her head, picking up a book, blowing her nose, and even taking her own life. In her book, *Joni, An Unforgettable Story*[72], she writes about her time of depression and how she wrestled through the core question of why God allows suffering. Joni says: "God permits what he hates, to accomplish what he loves. Her suffering," she continues, "has brought her closer to God. He hates spinal cord injury, yet he permits these things to accomplish things far more precious in our lives: a deeper relationship with God." It's been fifty years since her diving accident, and over the years she has learned to live with her disability, but now suffers from chronic pain. Her body, which doesn't feel or function the way she wants it to, is feeling. She can feel the pain. How unfair is that! Her legs won't bring her places, but keep her up at night in pain. And in bed, when she's not able to toss and turn, the pain is there, and the nights can be unbearable long and dark. A few years ago, Joni was diagnosed with breast cancer. She underwent a mastectomy, chemotherapy and radiation therapy. It was a difficult and intense journey, but the cancer went into remission. When she reached the five-year mark and was declared cancer-free, Ken— her husband—and herself were so relieved, as you can imagine. She told me how

---

[72] Joni Eareckson Tada *Joni, An Unforgettable Story* (United States: Zondervan, 1976)

people had asked her if it felt like "heaven on earth." She said it didn't. Not quite. "Because heaven on earth", she continued, "was during the sleepless nights of pain and worry. These dark and exhausting nights were where I met God. Where God met me. He found me and held me very close. When God meets you in the midst of your suffering, when He finds you in your hell, it's a splash of heaven, right there."

It reminds me of something King David said, some three thousand years ago: "You keep count of my tossings, you put my tears in your bottle. Are they not in you book?" (Psalm 56:8 ESV).

The pain and suffering in this world are overwhelming, unfair, and inevitable. In all the conversations around the world I had, I've heard many answers to and explanations for suffering. A lot of empty words, and well-meant promises, too. If I learned anything at all, it is this: that those who found peace in times of suffering were those who found something larger than the suffering.

Something bigger than life.

Someone who holds this world, and who will hold me.

That's why for me I found the answer in the questions of suffering in the promises of God. A God who cannot be shaken, and who sees all my tears.

HE HAS CHOSEN NOT TO HEAL ME

But to Hold me.

THE MORE INTENSE THE PAIN,
THE CLOSER HIS EMBRACE.

—JONI EARECKSON TADA

IN *A PLACE OF HEALING*: WRESTLING WITH THE MYSTERIES OF
SUFFERING, PAIN, AND GOD'S SOVEREIGNTY

DIG DEEP
The quest for water

*Ask and it will be given to you,
seek and you will find.
—Jesus[73]*

We did it! We dug and explored and made our one-foot holes. Now we know it all; about the different belief systems and all the choices we have. Well not all, we didn't go too deep, but enough to know what they stand for. There is a decision for you to make. You can stay here, or go deeper.

Lingering around the one-foot holes won't bring you much. To find water you need to dig deeper. As the Buddha said: six feet and beyond.

One of my favorite quotes is about striving, seeking and finding, without giving up. It's from Alfred, Lord Tennyson...

---

73 Matthew 7:7 NIV

TO STRIVE, TO SEEK, TO FIND, AND NOT TO YIELD

—Alfred, Lord Tennyson, "Ulysses"

Don't yield until you find what you're looking for. As we're coming to the end of this book, I want to tell you what I found as my truth, in my own quest for God or no god. But first one last story…

It was 1939, the dark and ominous days before the onset of World War II. To boost the morale of the people the British government ordered to design posters. The instructions were simple: The posters had to be plain, with a crystal-clear message of encouragement. And they had to carry the Tudor crown. Out of all the designs, King George VI chose three. They were soon to be found everywhere in Britain. Train stations, bus stops, shop windows, libraries, any public building—you name it, it had a poster on it. At least two of them. The third one was never used and slightly forgotten. Until a good sixty years later when a bookseller stumbled across a copy hidden among a pile of dusty old books. The rest is history because these words are now famous around the whole wide world. You could say it went totally viral, before viral was even a thing.

Keep Calm and Carry On. A heartening word to the Brits at dire times, but for us, in our spiritual journey, an easy way out. Don't worry, be happy, carpe diem, and you only live once—all that stuff. Do what you do, think, or believe, and don't make it too complicated. Life is what we make it to be, be nice, be happy. Keep calm and carry on...

The second of the posters is not so well known, but back in the day—in World War II—a common sight in Great Britain. It's the opposite of Keep Calm.

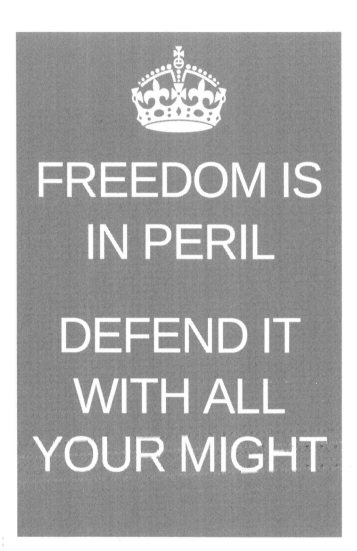

The two world wars have come and gone, and while writing this I'm safe and free. However, I know there is a battle going on, a spiritual battle for my soul. This battle makes the quest for God or no god so much more pressing than just a good feeling or the latest trend.

It's about the wholeness of my soul, the completeness of me as a person. This goes deeper than any made-up god or an inherited religion. That's why, in my humble opinion, and when it comes to matters of the heart, it's the dumbest advice ever to keep calm and carry on. We need to dig deeper. Our freedom is at stake, and we must fight for it with all we've got. It is about being whole. Not in peril, but complete.

Do Not Keep, Do Not Carry On.

Two posters, two options.

One life, your life.

In my own search for a god or no god, I'm a true antireligionist[74]. Not an atheist, because I've always believed in a higher power. As a young child I already had the sense that there was a god. I can't understand how there can be galaxies and snowflakes, apple-tree blossoms and symphonies, bright colors and bees, and the complexity of the human body without an intelligent designer. For me it can't be that an accidental series of events that caused this world to be. That's why there's always been a god for me.

The decision on *which* god to choose was made when I considered all the god-beliefs out there. I told you in

---

[74] My self-made-grammar-incorrect word, from page 104. But you get my point, right?

chapter three that once I thought I knew it all. I was brought up in a Christian family, with many good people around me. It made sense to me, so I became a Christian too. But when I grew older, and saw more of the pain in the world, and in my own life, it wasn't enough. It seemed too easy. David was plagued by doubt, a deep internal struggle of doubt by everything that he had seen in the world, and he questioned the sense to it all. Ruth struggled with depression and was overwhelmed with all the pain in the world. And that's when we had to dig for ourselves. Our 'inherited' faith wasn't enough to give us answers, and we had to seek and dig deeper. So we did. That's when we questioned, and explored the different god-beliefs. There was something going for each one of them, many similarities and good things to consider in all faiths, but in our own quest, we have chosen Jesus. And for a number of reasons[75].

---

[75] I diverted from my own 'I' and 'we' rule, because the struggle was very personal and not the same for both of us—just as it is with all of us. However our conclusion was mostly the same, so I will continue in the singular I—as in David + Ruth = I. Yep, just as the queen (see note on page 5).

Grace

Jesus was the only one who introduced me to grace. I didn't find grace in any of the other options. Most of them promised peace or an afterlife, but it always had to start with me, and would only come as a result of *my* works, *my* self-discipline, or *my* inner growth. I get that. After all, the gods are godly and I am not. I'm the lesser one, so I should climb, and work, and try, and do whatever I can to be worthy.

Jesus is different. He came to us and did it all. When He said: 'It's finished', right before He died on the cross it really was finished. All of it. He took away all my guilt and sin so I can come freely to God. This doesn't make sense to me, and it is not a fair trade. But I take it. I take it all.

It's undeserved and freely given. There's no greater grace.

I believe the void that we talked about earlier comes from our built-in need to be with God. It's in our bones; it's the only way to be whole. I don't think it can be filled by anything but God. And I'm blown away by the fact that God wants a relationship with me. As a father, a friend, a personal god. He wants this so badly that He gave His only Son. This goes way over my head, that God, the mighty Creator of the universe, wants me. That's amazing to me, this grace.

Amazing grace.

Peace

Another reason why I chose the God of the Bible is because I want peace. Duh. Who doesn't? Everybody wants peace. My yoga teacher this morning wished us all peace and said that the only way to find peace is to cultivate it within yourself. I would like that to be true, but it never really worked for me. At times I come really close, with mindfulness, discipline, and positive thinking—especially on good days. I've done that, I tried hard, but I couldn't keep it up. Life is so unpredictable, and in my experience self-cultivated peace was not enough to hold me when life got too hard. I rather take it from Someone larger than me. Someone who holds me, in this unpredictable life of mine.

Jesus said: "Peace I leave with you; my peace I give you, I do not give as the world gives. Do not let your hearts get troubled and do not be afraid". John 14:27 (NIV)

But don't take my word for it, try it for yourself. What is the most difficult part in your life, right now? Your biggest worry? The thing that keeps you up at night? It can be anything—big, small, overwhelming, or seemingly hopeless. Try it. Tell God.

In the Bible Paul[76] wrote: "Don't worry over anything whatever; tell God every detail of your needs in earnest and thankful prayer, and the peace of God which transcends human understanding, will keep constant guard over your hearts and minds as they rest in Christ Jesus". Philippians 4:6,7 (PHILIPS)

God promised peace, so ask for it. Another promise written in the Bible is that God will never leave you, nor forsake you, nor let you down (in Hebrews 13:5).

Love

And lastly love. God's unconditional love became the

---

[76] Paul (c.5-67)was an apostle (a teacher and follower of Jesus), who wrote a big part of the New Testament.

deciding factor for me. I couldn't find that anywhere else, not even close. I've seen love and beautiful things happen around the world. Sacrificing love, good love, but never this kind of love, not like Jesus. Someone who is without blame, gave His life for me,. That's a crazy, deep and unconditional love.

It's once more something I don't understand, because my human mind doesn't do unconditional very well. Jesus lived this kind of love.

Jesus never saw color, race, gender, or anything like that. He saw each person for who they really were. He was never afraid to be seen with the blind, the lame, the lepers—in that time the outcast of society.

Jesus saw them for who they truly were.

Kids at that time were often seen as a nuisance, but Jesus drew them close and saw their hearts.

In a world that ignored women, Jesus was different and treated them with respect and saw who they really were. One day the religious leaders brought a woman to Jesus. The woman was caught with another man, and according to the law she should be stoned to death. These leaders were the VIP's of their time, but Jesus didn't care. He saw right through their hypocrisy and told the leaders they should throw stones, if they were without fault. One by one disappeared.

Another day Jesus asked Zacchaeus[77] if he could have dinner at his house. This was unheard of, because Zacchaeus was a traitor. Again Jesus didn't care what others would say, He wanted to know what Zacchaeus had to say.

Jesus said that we should love our enemies, and that was exactly what He did. He helped a Roman officer (the oppressor), a Samaritan woman (a hostile neighboring nation,) and many more. Even on the cross, when Jesus died, He said to God: "Please, forgive them, for they do not know what do!"

---

[77] You can read about Jesus in the Bible- the book of John, in the New Testament is a good place to start reading about the life of Jesus.

That's Jesus. There's never anyone too low, too bad, or too insignificant for him. There is never anyone not good enough for Jesus.

Unlike religion, where you have to jump through all kinds of hoops to 'make' yourself presentable and good enough, Jesus did it all.

I believe that Jesus is the Son of God, and that He died for my sins. In Him I've found love, grace and a peace that's beyond understanding. There you have it. That's what I believe.

But what about you? What do you believe? Your decision is up to you.

Go now. Seek, question, and wonder. And find your water.

"But whoever drinks the water that I will give him will never become thirsty again. The water that I will give him will become a well of water for him, springing up to eternal life."

-Jesus, in John 4:14 (isv)

To stay up to date with OMG and be the first one to hear about book-signings, speaking-engagements and new projects from David Verboom and Ruth Schleppi-Verboom follow thebookOMG on Facebook or on Instagram.

Calabasas, November 26, 2017

84934616R00086

Made in the USA
San Bernardino, CA
15 August 2018